# List of Contents

# Introduction: The Art and Science of Contrarian Investing

In the ever-shifting landscape of finance and investment, where trends appear and disappear like fleeting shadows, the contrarian investor stands as a steadfast figure, charting an uncharted course. The allure of contrarian investing lies not in the comfort of conformity but in the daring pursuit of difference. It's a strategy that defies the crowd, challenges conventional wisdom, and, when wielded with skill and precision, can lead to exceptional profits. Welcome to "Contrarian Investing Strategy: How Being Different Can Boost Your Profits."

In the chapters that follow, we will embark on a journey into the heart of contrarian investing—a discipline that has shaped the fortunes of some of the greatest financial minds in history. Contrarian investing is, at its core, an art and science, a dance between instinct and analysis, and a testament to the power of individualism in the face of market noise.

## Understanding the Contrarian's Mindset

Before we delve into the depths of contrarian investing, it's essential to grasp the essence of the contrarian's mindset. Imagine a world where most are compelled to buy when stocks soar and sell when they plummet. The contrarian, on the other hand, resists the siren call of the crowd. When euphoria sweeps through the markets, the contrarian remains skeptical, seeking value in the overlooked and underappreciated. When panic descends, the contrarian sees opportunity amidst the chaos.

Contrarian investing is not for the faint of heart. It requires courage, conviction, and a keen sense of individualism. As we journey together through this book, you'll discover that a contrarian investor's path is often a lonely one. You'll face skepticism from peers who follow the herd and doubt from experts who tout the latest market trends. But remember this: it's precisely in the act of being different that your potential for profit truly emerges.

## The Contrarian's Advantage: Exploiting Market Inefficiencies

At its core, contrarian investing rests on a fundamental belief—the belief that markets are not always rational. While the Efficient Market Hypothesis (EMH) posits that stock prices fully reflect all available information, contrarian investors argue that emotions, biases, and collective behavior often lead to mispricing. It's in these mispriced assets that contrarian investors find their advantage.

Imagine, for a moment, a scenario where a stock that was once a market darling suddenly falls out of favor due to unforeseen circumstances. Traditional investors flee, selling their shares in a panic. The contrarian, however, remains calm, recognizing that the market's reaction may be overblown. Instead of following the crowd, the contrarian conducts rigorous analysis, seeking to determine if the company's fundamentals remain strong. If they do, the contrarian may see this as an opportunity to acquire shares at a discount, confident in the stock's potential for recovery.

## The Role of Behavioral Biases

Contrarian investing, at its heart, is an exercise in understanding and overcoming the psychological biases that drive market behavior. When the market rises, euphoria can lead investors to exhibit irrational exuberance, causing them to overlook warning signs and overvalue assets. Conversely, during downturns, fear and panic can trigger a cascade of selling, driving prices far below their intrinsic worth.

Here, the contrarian investor stands as a sentinel of reason, armed with the knowledge that emotions can distort perceptions of value. By studying and recognizing these cognitive biases, contrarians are better equipped to separate noise from signal and make informed, rational decisions.

## The Contrarian's Toolbox: Analytical and Emotional Resilience

Contrarian investing is not a simple matter of bucking the trend; it involves a sophisticated set of tools and techniques. From fundamental analysis that evaluates a company's financial health to technical analysis that identifies contrarian signals in stock charts, the contrarian's toolbox is diverse and dynamic.

However, tools alone do not make a contrarian investor successful. Emotional resilience plays an equally vital role. The ability to weather the storm of market volatility, to stand firm in the face of skepticism, and to trust one's analysis when the world seems to be heading in the opposite direction—these are the traits that set contrarian investors apart.

**A Glimpse of What Lies Ahead**

In the chapters that follow, we will take a deep dive into the world of contrarian investing. We will explore the strategies and tactics used by contrarians to uncover hidden gems in the market, to seize opportunities when others are gripped by fear, and to build portfolios that thrive in adversity.

From stock selection and market timing to risk management and global contrarian opportunities, each chapter will equip you with the practical knowledge and actionable insights needed to become a skilled contrarian investor. We will also examine real-life case studies of legendary contrarians, revealing the secrets of their success and the lessons they offer for modern investors.

Moreover, we will explore the evolving landscape of contrarian investing, from the integration of technology and data analytics to the consideration of environmental, social, and governance (ESG) factors in contrarian decision-making. We will also discuss the resources available to contrarian investors, from recommended reading materials to online tools and software that can enhance your contrarian strategies.

Finally, we will address advanced contrarian tactics for scaling your portfolio, optimizing tax efficiency, and building a lasting legacy. Contrarian investing is not just about profiting today; it's about securing your financial future and leaving a lasting impact.

As we embark on this journey together, keep in mind that contrarian investing is not a one-size-fits-all approach. It requires adaptability, continuous learning, and the courage to be different. Whether you're a seasoned investor seeking to refine your skills or a novice eager to learn the ropes, "Contrarian Investing Strategy" will be your trusted guide in the quest for greater profits and financial independence.

# Chapter 1: Understanding Contrarian Investing

## 1.1 What Is Contrarian Investing?

In the vast arena of investment strategies, there exists a method that defies convention and marches to the beat of its own drum—a strategy that has, over the years, produced legendary investors and outstanding returns. This strategy is none other than contrarian investing. In this sub chapter, we will dissect the very essence of contrarian investing—what it is, how it works, and why it matters.

### Definition and Concept

Contrarian investing, at its core, is a strategy that stands in stark contrast to the prevailing sentiment of the market. While the majority of investors tend to follow the herd, buying when optimism reigns and selling when pessimism abounds, contrarian investors chart a different course. They actively seek opportunities when others are fleeing, and they exercise caution when the masses are exuberant.

At its essence, contrarian investing embodies the principle of going against the crowd. It thrives on the belief that markets are not always rational and that emotional extremes can lead to mispricing of assets. Contrarians view market sentiment as a pendulum that swings between euphoria and despair, and they position themselves to benefit from these swings.

Imagine a scenario where a particular stock, once the darling of Wall Street, falls out of favor due to unexpected challenges. The broader market reacts with panic, leading to a sharp decline in the stock's price. While conventional investors might hastily sell their shares, contrarians seize this as an opportunity. They recognize that the market's reaction may be overblown and driven by emotion rather than fundamentals.

Contrarians will dive deep into the company's financials, assess its competitive position, and scrutinize its long-term prospects. If they find that the underlying business remains strong, they may choose to accumulate shares at a discounted price, confident that the market will eventually correct its mispricing.

Contrarian investing is not about blindly opposing popular sentiment; it's about rigorous analysis and calculated decisions. It's a strategy that requires a contrarian mindset—one that is willing to question the prevailing narrative, challenge the status quo, and, when necessary, stand apart from the crowd.

### Historical Success Stories

The annals of financial history are replete with the stories of contrarian investors who defied prevailing wisdom and reaped substantial rewards. These stories serve as both inspiration and evidence of the power of contrarian thinking.

One of the most celebrated contrarian investors in history is Sir John Templeton. During the depths of World War II, Templeton purchased 100 shares of every stock trading on the New York Stock Exchange that was priced at $1 per share or less, including many that were in bankruptcy. At a time when fear and uncertainty gripped the market, Templeton's contrarian move paid off handsomely, as the post-war recovery led to substantial gains.

Similarly, the name Warren Buffett is synonymous with contrarian success. Buffett's Berkshire Hathaway has a long history of investing in companies that are undervalued or facing adversity. His ability to see the potential in businesses that others shunned has earned him the moniker of "The Oracle of Omaha." Buffett's contrarian philosophy emphasizes the importance of buying when others are selling and staying the course even during turbulent times.

These historical success stories underscore a fundamental truth about contrarian investing: it has the potential to generate outsized returns precisely because it challenges the prevailing narrative. By having the courage to go against the tide, contrarian investors position themselves to benefit from market inefficiencies and misjudgments.

## Benefits and Risks

Contrarian investing offers a multitude of benefits for those who embrace it as a strategy. These advantages, however, come with their fair share of risks. To navigate this path successfully, one must be aware of both the potential rewards and the challenges.

Benefits of Contrarian Investing :

1. Profit Potential: Contrarian investors have the potential to buy undervalued assets and sell overvalued ones, leading to attractive returns.

2. Diversification: By going against market sentiment, contrarian investments often provide diversification benefits. When the broader market falters, contrarian holdings may remain resilient.

3. Long-Term Focus: Contrarians tend to focus on the long term. This perspective can help investors weather short-term market volatility and capitalize on opportunities that others may overlook.

4. Emotional Discipline: Contrarian investors learn to master their emotions, making decisions based on analysis rather than fear or greed. This discipline can lead to more rational investment choices.


Risks of Contrarian Investing :

1. Market Timing: Contrarian investing involves making bets on when market sentiment will shift. Timing the market can be challenging, and mistimed contrarian moves can lead to losses.

2. Uncertainty: Contrarians often invest in assets that are out of favor for a reason. These assets may carry higher levels of risk, including financial distress or industry challenges.

3. Psychological Resilience: Contrarian investors must possess the psychological fortitude to stand apart from the crowd, even in the face of criticism and skepticism. This can be emotionally taxing.

4. Limited Liquidity: Some contrarian investments may lack liquidity, making it challenging to enter or exit positions, especially with large sums of capital.

Understanding the benefits and risks of contrarian investing is crucial for anyone considering this strategy. Contrarian investing is not a guarantee of success, but when applied with discipline and sound analysis, it can offer a unique path to potentially greater profits and financial resilience.

## 1.2 The Psychology Behind Contrarian Investing

In the fast-paced world of finance, the concept of contrarian investing has long been a beacon of hope for those who seek to outperform the market. It's a strategy that stands in stark contrast to the prevailing sentiment, one that often rewards the bold and the unconventional. To truly grasp the essence of contrarian investing, we must delve into the intricate realm of psychology—the invisible force that shapes our perceptions, decisions, and ultimately, our financial destinies.

## Herd Mentality vs. Contrarian Thinking

Picture a bustling stock market, where traders and investors move in unison, their actions seemingly synchronized. This is the manifestation of herd mentality—the human tendency to follow the crowd. It's a phenomenon deeply ingrained in our psychology, dating back to our primitive ancestors, who relied on group cohesion for survival. In the financial realm, however, herd mentality often leads to suboptimal outcomes.

When the majority rushes to buy a particular stock, it can inflate its price to unsustainable levels, creating bubbles that eventually burst. Conversely, when panic ensues, and everyone rushes for the exit, it can lead to indiscriminate selling and market crashes. Herd mentality, while providing a sense of safety in numbers, can be the downfall of many investors.

Contrarian thinking, on the other hand, is the deliberate act of going against the herd. It's the recognition that markets can become overly optimistic or pessimistic, leading to mispricing. Contrarians believe that the crowd is not always right and are willing to challenge the prevailing sentiment. They seek value in the neglected, the unloved, and the overlooked.

## Behavioral Biases to Overcome

To become a successful contrarian investor, one must first acknowledge the influence of behavioral biases on decision-making. These biases are the product of our evolutionary heritage, often leading us astray in the complex world of finance.

Confirmation bias, for instance, is the tendency to seek out information that confirms our preexisting beliefs while ignoring or dismissing contradictory data. In investing, this can lead to a dangerous echo chamber where we only hear what we want to hear. Contrarians actively combat confirmation bias by seeking diverse opinions and considering alternative viewpoints.

Another common bias is loss aversion, the irrational fear of losses that can lead to premature selling or reluctance to take necessary risks. Contrarians understand that losses are an inherent part of investing and are often the price of admission to potentially significant gains.

Overcoming these biases is not easy, but it's a critical aspect of developing a contrarian mindset. It requires self-awareness, discipline, and a willingness to challenge your own instincts.

## Developing a Contrarian Mindset

A contrarian mindset is not something one is born with; rather, it's a skill that can be cultivated over time. It begins with recognizing that the majority may not always be right and that markets can be influenced by emotions and irrational behavior.

To develop a contrarian mindset, start by embracing skepticism. When the crowd is exuberant about a particular investment or asset class, question the basis for their enthusiasm. Likewise, when fear and panic grip the markets, take a step back and assess whether the situation warrants such extreme reactions.

Contrarians also practice the art of independent thinking. They are not swayed by the opinions of the masses or the noise of financial news networks. Instead, they conduct thorough research, analyze data objectively, and form their own conclusions.

Patience is another cornerstone of the contrarian mindset. Contrarians understand that it may take time for the market to recognize the value they see in an asset. They are willing to wait for the right moment to strike, even if it means swimming against the current for an extended period.

Moreover, contrarians embrace the concept of contrarian indicators. These are signals that suggest the prevailing sentiment is reaching an extreme and may be due for a reversal. Contrarian indicators can range from the level of bullishness or bearishness in the market to specific technical patterns. Recognizing these signs can provide valuable insights into potential opportunities.

Understanding the psychology behind contrarian investing is not just about recognizing the flaws in human behavior but also about harnessing those insights to make informed and rational decisions. Contrarian thinking is a powerful tool for investors who seek to outperform the crowd and achieve exceptional results in the world of finance. In the following chapters, we will delve deeper into the practical strategies and techniques that contrarian investors use to turn these principles into profitable actions.

## 1.3 Why Contrarian Investing Works

In the world of finance, where theories and strategies abound, the concept of contrarian investing stands as a bold and audacious counterpoint to the prevailing wisdom. It challenges the notion that markets are always rational and efficient, offering a compelling alternative perspective— one that suggests that the very inefficiencies and irrationalities of the market can be harnessed to achieve superior returns.

### Efficient Market Hypothesis and Its Critiques

To understand why contrarian investing works, we must first confront the cornerstone theory of modern finance: the Efficient Market Hypothesis (EMH). Proposed by Eugene F. Fama in the 1960s, the EMH posits that financial markets are perfectly efficient. In an efficient market, asset prices always reflect all available information. Therefore, it is impossible to consistently outperform the market through active trading or stock selection because any new information is rapidly and accurately incorporated into prices.

The EMH comes in three forms: weak, semi-strong, and strong. The weak form asserts that past price and volume information is already reflected in current prices. The semi-strong form extends this to include all publicly available information, while the strong form encompasses all information, including private information known only to insiders.

While the EMH has been influential in shaping financial theory and practice, it has also faced significant criticism and skepticism. Critics argue that markets are not perfectly efficient, and there are several reasons to question the EMH's assumptions.

1. Behavioral Biases: One of the most compelling critiques of the EMH is the existence of behavioral biases in market participants. Humans are not always rational decision-makers. They can be influenced by emotions, cognitive biases, and herd behavior. These psychological factors can lead to mispricing of assets, creating opportunities for contrarian investors.

2. Limits to Arbitrage: The EMH assumes that arbitrage—buying undervalued assets and selling overvalued assets—eliminates any discrepancies in prices. However, there are limits to arbitrage due to transaction costs, short-selling constraints, and behavioral biases among market participants. These limits can prevent arbitrageurs from quickly correcting mispricings.

3. Market Inefficiencies: Markets are complex systems influenced by a multitude of factors, including news, sentiment, and investor behavior. These factors can create inefficiencies in the short term, as market participants may overreact or underreact to information. Contrarian investors

seek to exploit these inefficiencies by betting against the prevailing sentiment.

In essence, contrarian investing challenges the efficient market hypothesis by recognizing that markets are not always perfectly efficient, and that mispricings and overreactions occur due to human behavior and market dynamics. Contrarians take advantage of these imperfections to identify opportunities for profit.

**Market Inefficiencies to Exploit**

Contrarian investing thrives on the idea that markets are inherently imperfect and that inefficiencies can persist over time. To understand why contrarian strategies work, it's essential to explore some of the key market inefficiencies that contrarians seek to exploit:

1. Overreaction and Underreaction: Investors often react emotionally to news and events, causing overreactions in asset prices. For instance, a negative earnings report can lead to a sharp sell-off, even if the company's long-term prospects remain sound. Conversely, underreactions occur when investors fail to fully incorporate new information, resulting in slow price adjustments.

2. Momentum and Trend Reversals: Market trends, both upward and downward, can persist for some time. However, they are not infinite. Contrarian investors look for signs that a trend is nearing exhaustion, anticipating trend reversals. This strategy involves selling during euphoric market rallies and buying during market panics.

3. Neglected and Unpopular Assets: Markets often overlook or undervalue certain assets or sectors. Contrarian investors actively seek out these neglected opportunities, believing that market sentiment will eventually catch up with their analysis, leading to price corrections.

4. Market Cycles: Markets move in cycles, from bull markets to bear markets and back again. Contrarian investors recognize that market sentiment tends to be most extreme at market peaks and troughs. By going against the prevailing sentiment, they aim to profit from the eventual market reversals.


**Historical Performance Data**
To appreciate the efficacy of contrarian investing, we can turn to historical performance data, which provides compelling evidence of its success. Contrarian strategies have yielded impressive returns in various market conditions and asset classes.

Consider the following historical examples:

1. Value Investing: Pioneered by contrarian legends Benjamin Graham and Warren Buffett, value investing involves buying undervalued stocks with the expectation that their true value will be recognized by the market over time. The long-term success of value investors serves as a testament to the effectiveness of contrarian principles.

2. Bear Market Recoveries: During bear markets, when pessimism reigns, contrarian investors often find opportunities to buy quality assets at deeply discounted

prices. The subsequent recoveries in these assets can result in substantial gains.

3. Dot-Com Bubble: The bursting of the dot-com bubble in the early 2000s was a stark reminder of the dangers of speculative investing. Contrarians who recognized the excesses of the tech boom and took defensive positions ahead of the crash were well-positioned to capitalize on the subsequent market recovery.

4. Financial Crises: Contrarian strategies have proven valuable during financial crises, such as the 2008 global financial crisis. Investors who had the courage to enter the market when fear was rampant were rewarded as markets rebounded.

These historical instances underscore the resilience and profitability of contrarian investing. While it is not without its challenges and risks, contrarian investing offers a time-tested approach for investors willing to think independently and swim against the current of popular opinion.

# Chapter 2: Building Your Contrarian Investment Strategy

## 2.1 Setting Your Investment Goals

In the world of contrarian investing, where the road less traveled often leads to the greatest rewards, your journey begins with a clear sense of direction. Just as a skilled navigator sets a course before embarking on a voyage, a successful contrarian investor defines their investment goals to guide their path. In this subchapter, we will explore the essential elements of setting your investment goals—a critical first step in crafting a contrarian strategy that aligns with your aspirations, risk tolerance, and time horizon.

### Defining Short-term and Long-term Objectives

Contrarian investing is not a one-size-fits-all endeavor; it's a flexible framework that adapts to your unique financial circumstances and ambitions. To embark on your contrarian journey, start by defining your investment objectives, which can generally be categorized into short-term and long-term goals.

Short-term Objectives: These are the financial milestones you aim to achieve in the relatively near future. They could include saving for a down payment on a home, funding your child's education, or accumulating an emergency fund. Short-term goals often have a time horizon of a few months to a few years.

Long-term Objectives: Long-term goals extend further into the future, typically beyond five years. Examples of long-term objectives include retirement planning, building wealth over several decades, or leaving a financial legacy for your heirs.

When defining your objectives, be as specific as possible. Rather than merely stating, "I want to retire comfortably," consider setting a target retirement age, estimating the income you'll need, and determining the lifestyle you desire in retirement. Specificity helps transform vague aspirations into concrete goals, making it easier to measure progress and develop a contrarian strategy tailored to your needs.

**Risk Tolerance Assessment**

Contrarian investing, while potentially rewarding, is not without its share of risks. Before devising your strategy, it's crucial to assess your tolerance for risk. Risk tolerance is a deeply personal characteristic influenced by factors such as your financial situation, psychological disposition, and time horizon.

Contrarian investors often embrace higher levels of risk by challenging market consensus and investing against prevailing sentiment. However, this doesn't mean recklessness; it means calculated risk-taking. To gauge your risk tolerance:

1. Financial Capacity: Assess your financial stability, including your income, expenses, debt obligations, and emergency savings. A solid financial foundation can provide a buffer against market volatility.

2. Emotional Resilience: Consider your ability to withstand market fluctuations without emotional distress. If the thought of a market downturn keeps you up at night, you may have a lower risk tolerance and need to adjust your strategy accordingly.

3. Investment Horizon: Longer investment horizons typically allow for greater risk-taking, as there is more time to recover from potential losses. Shorter horizons may necessitate a more conservative approach.

4. Diversification: Evaluate your existing portfolio, if any, and its level of diversification. A well-diversified portfolio can help manage risk, as different assets may respond differently to market conditions.

5. Goals and Aspirations: Consider how your investment objectives align with your risk tolerance. Are you willing to accept higher volatility for the potential of greater returns, or do you prioritize capital preservation?

6. Historical Perspective: Reflect on past investment experiences and how you reacted to market fluctuations. Your past behavior can offer insights into your risk tolerance.

Once you've assessed your risk tolerance, you can categorize yourself as a conservative, moderate, or aggressive investor. This categorization will inform the risk level you are comfortable with when implementing your contrarian strategy.

**Asset Allocation Strategy**

With your investment objectives and risk tolerance clarified, the next step in building your contrarian investment strategy is defining your asset allocation strategy. Asset allocation refers to the distribution of your investment capital among various asset classes, such as stocks, bonds, real estate, and alternative investments. It's a pivotal decision that significantly influences your portfolio's risk and return characteristics.

The key principle of contrarian asset allocation is diversification. Diversifying your investments across different asset classes can help reduce risk by spreading exposure. Contrarian investors often favor a balanced approach that includes a mix of traditional and non-traditional assets. Here's how to approach asset allocation:

1. Assess Your Risk-Return Trade-off: Your risk tolerance should guide your asset allocation decisions. Aggressive investors may allocate a larger portion of their portfolio to higher-risk, higher-reward assets like stocks, while conservative investors may favor bonds and stable assets.

2. Consider Your Investment Horizon: Longer time horizons permit more aggressive asset allocations, as you have the luxury of waiting out market fluctuations. Short-term goals may necessitate a more conservative allocation to protect capital.

3. Diversify Across Asset Classes: Diversification is a contrarian's best friend. Allocate your investments across a mix of asset classes to reduce the impact of downturns in any one sector. Consider stocks, bonds, real estate,

commodities, and even alternative investments like private equity or hedge funds.

4. Rebalance Periodically: Over time, your portfolio's asset allocation may drift from your original targets due to market movements. Regularly review and rebalance your portfolio to maintain your desired allocation and risk level.

5. Factor in Economic Conditions: Contrarian investors pay close attention to macroeconomic conditions and market sentiment. In times of economic uncertainty, they may adjust their asset allocation to capitalize on potential contrarian opportunities.

6. Seek Professional Guidance: If you're uncertain about asset allocation or lack the expertise to make informed decisions, consider consulting a financial advisor with experience in contrarian strategies.


Your asset allocation strategy is the backbone of your contrarian investment plan. It should reflect your unique financial circumstances, risk tolerance, and investment goals. By thoughtfully constructing your asset allocation, you lay the groundwork for a portfolio that can weather market storms while pursuing your desired returns.

## 2.2 Stock Selection for Contrarian Investors

In the stock market, where fortunes rise and fall with the ebb and flow of economic tides, one of the defining moments for contrarian investors is the selection of stocks. Stock selection, while integral to all investment strategies, takes on a unique significance in the contrarian's playbook. To become a master of contrarian investing, one must first learn the art of identifying out-of-favor stocks, mastering fundamental analysis techniques, and deciphering the intricate language of technical analysis and contrarian signals.

### Identifying Out-of-Favor Stocks

Contrarian investors thrive in the shadows of the market, where the mainstream spotlight often fails to shine. For this reason, the first step in stock selection for contrarians is identifying those companies that have fallen out of favor with the broader investment community. These stocks, often neglected or abandoned, can hold hidden gems waiting to be unearthed.

But how does one identify these out-of-favor stocks amidst the bustling marketplace? Contrarians look for specific characteristics that set these stocks apart:

* Negative Sentiment: Out-of-favor stocks are typically accompanied by a chorus of pessimism. Negative news headlines, analyst downgrades, and general market sentiment all point to stocks that are out of favor.

* Low Price-to-Earnings (P/E) Ratios: Stocks trading at low P/E ratios relative to their historical averages or industry peers may be overlooked by investors who favor growth and momentum stocks.

* Underperformance: Stocks that have underperformed the broader market or their sector for an extended period may be candidates for contrarian interest.

* Contrarian Literature: Contrarian investors also delve into contrarian literature, exploring books and research that spotlight undervalued stocks and industries. They look for insights that challenge conventional wisdom.

Once out-of-favor stocks have been identified, contrarian investors turn their attention to the art of analysis.

**Fundamental Analysis Techniques**
Contrarian stock selection is grounded in the fundamentals of a company. Here, it's essential to distinguish between the short-term noise of market sentiment and the long-term prospects of a business. Fundamental analysis provides the tools to make this distinction.

* Earnings and Revenue Growth: Contrarians examine a company's historical earnings and revenue growth to assess its financial health. A history of consistent growth, even if recently interrupted, can be a sign of a resilient business.

* Balance Sheet Strength: A solid balance sheet is the bedrock of a company's financial stability. Contrarians

scrutinize a company's debt levels, cash reserves, and current assets to ensure it can weather economic storms.

* Competitive Advantage: Companies with a sustainable competitive advantage, often referred to as a "moat," are more likely to thrive in the long term. Contrarians seek businesses with unique strengths that insulate them from competition.

* Valuation Metrics: Contrarian investors are known for their value-oriented approach. They look for stocks trading below their intrinsic value, often employing metrics like the Price-to-Earnings (P/E) ratio, Price-to-Book (P/B) ratio, and Price-to-Sales (P/S) ratio.

Fundamental analysis is not about making short-term predictions but rather about assessing a company's long-term potential. It's a sober examination of the company's financial health and competitive position, free from the influence of market sentiment.


**Technical Analysis and Contrarian Signals**
While fundamental analysis provides a solid foundation for stock selection, contrarian investors recognize that market sentiment can sometimes swing excessively, leading to mispricing. This is where technical analysis and contrarian signals come into play. Contrarian investors use technical indicators to gauge market sentiment and identify potential turning points.

* Relative Strength Index (RSI): The RSI measures the speed and change of price movements. An RSI below 30 is

often seen as an oversold signal, suggesting that the stock may be due for a rebound.

* Moving Averages: Contrarians pay close attention to moving averages, particularly the 200-day moving average. When a stock's price falls below its 200-day moving average, it can signal a shift in market sentiment.

* Volume Analysis: A surge in trading volume, especially on a down day, can indicate capitulation—when investors give up on a stock. Contrarians may view this as a potential buying opportunity.

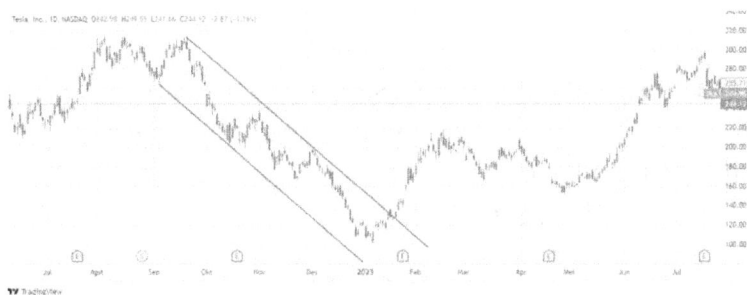

**Figure 1 (Tesla Stock show decline until 2023 when they slowly rebound)**

* Contrarian Indicators: Some technical indicators are specifically designed for contrarian investors. For example, the Arms Index (TRIN) compares advancing and declining issues to assess market sentiment. A TRIN above 2 is often considered a contrarian buy signal.

It's important to note that technical analysis is not without its controversies and detractors. Critics argue that it relies

27

on past price movements and patterns, which may not always accurately predict future market behavior. Contrarians, however, view technical analysis as another tool in their arsenal, providing insights into market sentiment that may not be evident from fundamental analysis alone.

Stock selection for contrarian investors is a multifaceted process that combines the art of identifying out-of-favor stocks with the science of fundamental and technical analysis. It's a careful consideration between recognizing opportunities that others overlook and assessing a company's true worth.

## 2.3  Timing Your Contrarian Moves

In the world of contrarian investing, timing is everything. While the essence of contrarian philosophy revolves around going against the crowd, it's not a reckless charge into the unknown. Rather, it's a strategic and well-timed entry into opportunities that others may not yet recognize. In this subchapter, we'll delve into the critical aspects of timing your contrarian moves, understanding market cycles, utilizing essential tools, and managing risks along the way.

## Market Cycles and Contrarian Opportunities

Contrarian investing thrives on the cyclical nature of markets. Understanding these cycles and their phases is pivotal in identifying contrarian opportunities. Let's break down the primary market cycles and how they intersect with contrarian strategies:

1. Bull Markets: Bull markets are periods of sustained optimism and rising asset prices. Contrarian investors remain cautious during bull markets, as euphoria can lead to overvaluation. However, they also keep an eye out for signs of excessive exuberance, as this can signal an impending reversal. Contrarians may start building cash positions and researching undervalued assets during this phase.

2. Bear Markets: Bear markets are characterized by declining prices and pessimism. Contrarians thrive in these environments. They look for assets that have been unfairly punished, often due to fear or panic. This is when contrarians deploy their cash reserves to acquire assets at discounted prices, anticipating future recoveries.

3. Correction Phases: Corrections are shorter-term market declines within a broader bull market. Contrarians view corrections as opportunities to add to their positions in fundamentally strong assets that have temporarily dipped in value. They see corrections as healthy for markets, preventing bubbles from forming.

4. Sideways or Range-Bound Markets: Sometimes, markets neither surge nor plummet but move within a narrow range. Contrarians may stay patient during these times, waiting for

clearer signals of undervaluation or overvaluation. They focus on assets with strong fundamentals that can withstand the uncertainty.

## Tools for Timing Contrarian Buys and Sells

Contrarian investing isn't guesswork; it's a calculated approach that relies on data and analysis. Here are essential tools contrarians use to time their moves effectively:

1. Technical Analysis: Contrarians employ technical analysis to identify potential buy and sell signals. They examine price charts, moving averages, support and resistance levels, and other indicators to gauge the sentiment and momentum of an asset. Contrarians often look for oversold conditions or divergence between price and momentum indicators as signs of potential contrarian opportunities.

2. Fundamental Analysis: While contrarian investors may use technical analysis, they never disregard the fundamentals. In fact, fundamental analysis is at the core of their decision-making process. They assess financial statements, earnings reports, and economic data to determine the intrinsic value of an asset. Contrarians seek assets trading below their intrinsic value and look for catalysts that could drive a price correction.

3. Contrarian Indicators: Contrarian investors have developed unique indicators that help them identify when sentiment has reached extreme levels. For example, the put/call ratio, which measures options trading sentiment,

can indicate when investors are overly bearish (contrarian buy signal) or excessively bullish (contrarian sell signal).

4. Sentiment Analysis: Contrarians pay close attention to market sentiment. They read financial news, analyze social media chatter, and monitor sentiment surveys. When the majority of investors are pessimistic, contrarians see potential for a contrarian buy opportunity, and vice versa.

## Risk Management in Contrarian Trading

Contrarian investing, like any form of investing, carries risks. To mitigate these risks, contrarians employ various risk management strategies:

1. Diversification: Contrarian investors often diversify their portfolios to spread risk. Diversification involves holding a mix of assets across different industries or sectors. By doing so, contrarians reduce the impact of poor performance in one area.

2. Stop-Loss Orders: Contrarians use stop-loss orders to limit potential losses. These orders automatically sell a position if it reaches a predetermined price level. It's a way to prevent a small loss from turning into a significant one.

3. Position Sizing: Controlling the size of each position is crucial. Contrarians avoid putting all their capital into a single asset, ensuring that a poor-performing investment doesn't devastate their overall portfolio.

4. Continuous Monitoring: Contrarian investors keep a watchful eye on their investments and the overall market.

They adjust their positions as new information emerges or as market conditions change.

5. Patience: Contrarians understand that not every contrarian move will yield immediate results. They exhibit patience, waiting for their theses to play out, even if it takes time for the market to recognize the value they see.

6. Risk-Reward Assessment: Before making any contrarian move, investors assess the potential risk and reward. They weigh the upside potential against the downside risk, ensuring that the potential reward justifies the risk taken.

Contrarian investing is not a hasty endeavor; it's a strategic approach that combines careful analysis, timing, and risk management. By mastering the art of timing your contrarian moves, you position yourself to capitalize on market inefficiencies and potentially unlock significant profits. Remember, in the world of contrarian investing, patience and discipline are your allies, and calculated risk-taking is your path to success.

# Chapter 3: Analyzing Market Sentiment

## 3.1 Understanding Market Sentiment

In the vast arena of financial markets, understanding market sentiment is akin to deciphering the code of human emotion—a code that often defies logic and reason. Yet, within the realm of contrarian investing, comprehending and harnessing market sentiment is essential. In this subchapter, we'll explore the nuances of market sentiment, from its various types and how it wields influence over asset prices to the invaluable contrarian indicators that guide us in this intricate dance.

### Types of Market Sentiment

Market sentiment, like the tides of the ocean, is ever-changing, driven by a multitude of factors. It is the collective mood of investors and traders, a psychological force that can swing markets dramatically. To navigate this terrain, we must first understand the different types of market sentiment:

1. Bullish Sentiment: When optimism reigns supreme, and investors are bullish, they have a positive outlook on the market or a particular asset. Bullish sentiment is often marked by a belief in rising prices, increased buying activity, and a willingness to take on risk.

2. Bearish Sentiment: Conversely, bearish sentiment prevails when pessimism dominates. Investors with bearish sentiments anticipate falling prices, leading to heightened selling, risk aversion, and a general sense of caution.

3. Neutral Sentiment: Not all market participants fall into either the bullish or bearish camp. Neutral sentiment reflects a state of uncertainty or indifference, where investors are neither overly optimistic nor pessimistic. They may adopt . "wait and see" approach.

4. Extreme Sentiment: Markets are not always in a state of equilibrium. Extreme sentiment occurs when a significant portion of investors becomes overly bullish or bearish. These extremes often precede reversals, as sentiment reaches unsustainable levels.

5. Contrarian Sentiment: Contrarian sentiment is a subset of extreme sentiment. Contrarian investors seek opportunities when market sentiment reaches extremes. For instance, if the majority of investors are extremely bearish, contrarians view this as a potential buying opportunity.


**How Sentiment Influences Prices**
Market sentiment is not merely a reflection of investors' emotions; it is a force that influences asset prices in tangible ways. Understanding this influence is key to successful contrarian investing. Here's how sentiment can sway prices:

1. Momentum Buying and Selling: Bullish sentiment can fuel momentum buying, where investors rush to buy assets, driving prices higher. Conversely, bearish sentiment can lead to momentum selling, causing a cascade of selling pressure and price declines.

2. Overvaluation and Undervaluation: Sentiment can lead to overvaluation or undervaluation of assets. Bullish sentiment may push prices far above their intrinsic value, while bearish sentiment can cause prices to drop well below their true worth.

3. Herd Behavior: Investors often follow the crowd, especially in moments of extreme sentiment. Herd behavior can exaggerate price movements, as the majority rushes to buy or sell based on sentiment rather than fundamentals.

4. Market News and Media Influence: Sentiment can be amplified by the media's coverage of market events. Positive or negative news can magnify the sentiment, leading to rapid price movements.

5. Feedback Loops: Sentiment can create feedback loops. Rising prices can lead to increased bullish sentiment, which drives prices higher. Conversely, falling prices can intensify bearish sentiment, leading to further declines.

## Contrarian Indicators

Contrarian investing hinges on identifying moments when market sentiment has swung to extremes, offering contrarian investors opportunities to go against the crowd. Several contrarian indicators serve as valuable tools in this endeavor:

1. Put/Call Ratio: This ratio measures options trading sentiment. A high put/call ratio suggests excessive bearishness and may signal a contrarian buying opportunity.

2. Volatility Index (VIX): The VIX, often referred to as the "fear gauge," measures market volatility. Extreme spikes in the VIX can indicate heightened fear and potential contrarian buy signals.

3. Breadth Indicators: These indicators assess the number of advancing and declining stocks in the market. A disproportionate number of declining stocks, coupled with extreme bearish sentiment, can signal contrarian buying opportunities.

4. Investor Sentiment Surveys: Surveys that gauge investor sentiment can provide valuable insights. When surveys show extreme pessimism, it may signal a contrarian opportunity.

5. CBOE Equity Put/Call Ratio: This ratio focuses on equity options and can reveal whether investors are overloading on bearish bets.

6. Short Interest: Monitoring the level of short interest in a stock or asset can highlight contrarian opportunities. A high level of short interest may lead to a short squeeze if sentiment reverses.

Understanding these contrarian indicators and recognizing when they align with extreme market sentiment is a skill that contrarian investors cultivate. It allows them to make informed decisions that defy the prevailing sentiment, potentially leading to profitable outcomes.

In the herd of market sentiment, contrarian investors emerge as the navigators, reading the currents and tides of emotion with precision. By comprehending the types of sentiment, acknowledging its influence on prices, and harnessing the power of contrarian indicators, you, too, can embark on the contrarian path—a path where the contrarian sentiment is your guiding star in the vast sea of financial markets.

## 3.2 Monitoring News and Social Media

In the realm of contrarian investing, staying informed is paramount. Effective monitoring of news and social media can serve as your compass in navigating the intricate web of financial markets. It's not just about being up-to-date; it's about harnessing the power of information to gain a competitive edge. In this subchapter, we will explore the strategies and techniques contrarian investors employ to leverage news and social sentiment, the indispensable tools and resources at their disposal, and how to strike the right balance to avoid information overload.

### Leveraging News and Social Sentiment

The financial markets are a dynamic ecosystem influenced by an intricate interplay of factors, and news and social sentiment are two potent elements in this mix. Contrarian investors understand that the crowd's perception of news can be as important as the news itself. Here's how contrarians leverage these forces:

1. Contrarian Analysis of News: Contrarians approach news with a critical eye. They recognize that media narratives can sometimes exaggerate market movements, leading to overreactions. Instead of blindly following headlines, they scrutinize the underlying data and assess whether the market's response is justified.

2. Anticipating Market Sentiment: Contrarians often anticipate how the market will react to news. If they believe the market will overreact to negative news, they might see it as an opportunity to buy undervalued assets. Conversely, if they anticipate euphoria following positive news, they might prepare to take profits or establish short positions.

3. Contrarian Signals from Social Media: Social media platforms have become a hub of financial discussions. Contrarian investors monitor platforms like Twitter, Reddit, and financial forums to gauge sentiment. Sudden spikes in discussions, positive or negative, can be contrarian signals. However, they exercise caution, as social media sentiment can be subject to manipulation.

## Tools and Resources for Tracking News

To stay ahead of the curve, contrarian investors rely on a multitude of tools and resources designed to filter the noise and extract actionable insights from the constant flow of information. Here are some essential tools and techniques:

1. News Aggregators: Contrarian investors often use news aggregator platforms that compile news from various sources. These platforms allow them to quickly scan headlines and identify critical stories. Popular news aggregators include Google News, Bloomberg, and Reuters.

2. Real-Time News Feeds: Contrarians subscribe to real-time news feeds that provide up-to-the-minute updates on market events. These feeds can be integrated into trading platforms or accessed through dedicated news services, ensuring that no significant development is missed.

3. Sentiment Analysis Tools: Advanced sentiment analysis tools use natural language processing algorithms to assess the sentiment of news articles and social media posts. These tools help contrarians gauge whether the prevailing sentiment is bullish, bearish, or neutral.

4. Customized Alerts: Many contrarian investors set up customized news alerts based on specific keywords or criteria. This ensures they receive notifications when news that's relevant to their investments breaks, allowing for rapid response.

5. Financial News Websites: Contrarians regularly visit trusted financial news websites, such as CNBC, Bloomberg, and Financial Times. These sites provide in-depth analysis, expert opinions, and interviews with industry leaders, offering a comprehensive view of market events.

## Avoiding Information Overload

In the digital age, information flows incessantly, and it's easy to succumb to information overload. Contrarian investors are acutely aware of this challenge and employ strategies to maintain clarity amidst the noise:

1. Focus on Quality over Quantity: Contrarians prioritize the quality of information over its quantity. They avoid indiscriminate consumption of news and instead select sources known for accuracy and reliability.

2. Set Clear Objectives: Before diving into news and social media, contrarians establish clear objectives. They define what specific information they are seeking and what actions they might take based on that information. This focus helps prevent distraction.

3. Scheduled Information Consumption: Rather than being constantly tethered to news feeds, contrarians allocate specific times for information consumption. This approach prevents them from being overwhelmed by the constant influx of data.

4. Filter Noise from Signal: Contrarians develop the skill of discerning noise from signal. They are selective in what they pay attention to and discard information that lacks relevance or impact on their investment thesis.

5. Maintain a Contrarian Perspective: Contrarians remember their unique perspective in the face of market consensus. This mindset allows them to sift through information with a discerning eye, seeking opportunities where others see chaos.

In the world of contrarian investing, the ability to harness news and social sentiment is a potent weapon. It enables investors to position themselves ahead of the curve, identify undervalued assets, and make informed decisions. However, mastering this skill requires discipline, discernment, and a steadfast commitment to maintaining clarity in the face of information overload. As we continue on this journey of contrarian investing, remember that your ability to leverage information effectively can be the key to unlocking profitable opportunities.

## 3.3 Filtering Noise from Signals

In the intricate world of contrarian investing, where perception can often outweigh reality, the ability to separate noise from signal becomes a paramount skill. Market sentiment, while a valuable source of insight, is often shrouded in layers of irrationality and herd behavior. In this subchapter, we will embark on a journey into the realm of filtering noise from signals, a pivotal step in harnessing the power of sentiment data for your contrarian investment strategy.

### Critical Analysis of Sentiment Data

Market sentiment, like a tempestuous sea, can be both a blessing and a curse for investors. It can provide early indications of market shifts, but it can also lead to hasty decisions based on emotion rather than analysis. Critical analysis is your lifeboat in this turbulent sea.

1. Source Evaluation: Not all sentiment sources are created equal. In the digital age, sentiment data floods in from various channels, including financial news, social media, and surveys. Critical analysis begins with evaluating the credibility and reliability of your chosen sources. Are they known for accurate reporting, or are they prone to sensationalism? Distinguishing reliable sources from unreliable ones is the first step in filtering sentiment noise.

2. Time Frame Considerations: Sentiment data varies in time frames, from short-term intraday sentiment to longer-term investor sentiment. Different time frames can yield conflicting signals. Contrarian investors must carefully choose the time frame that aligns with their investment horizon and strategy.

3. Sentiment Analysis Tools: Leveraging sentiment analysis tools and software can be a game-changer. These tools use natural language processing and machine learning algorithms to sift through vast amounts of data and gauge sentiment. They can help identify patterns and trends that human analysis alone may overlook.

4. Historical Data: Examining historical sentiment data can provide valuable context. How did sentiment behave in similar market conditions in the past? Understanding historical patterns can help you filter out transient noise and focus on more significant signals.

5. Sentiment Relevance: Not all sentiment data is relevant to your investment thesis. You must filter out irrelevant noise by focusing on the sentiment directly related to the assets or sectors you are interested in. For example, if you're investing in tech stocks, sentiment about the healthcare sector may not be pertinent.

## Combining Sentiment with Other Indicators

Filtering noise from sentiment signals is just the beginning. The true power of sentiment analysis emerges when it is combined with other indicators to form a comprehensive investment strategy.

1. Technical Indicators: Contrarian investors often integrate sentiment analysis with technical indicators. By pairing sentiment data with charts and technical signals, you can confirm or contradict the sentiment-driven narrative. For example, if sentiment is overwhelmingly bearish, but technical indicators suggest an oversold condition, it may indicate a potential contrarian buying opportunity.

2. Fundamental Analysis: Fundamentals remain the backbone of contrarian investing. Combining sentiment data with fundamental analysis can lead to well-informed decisions. If sentiment is negative, but the company's financials remain strong, it may suggest an undervalued opportunity.

3. Market Breadth: Market breadth indicators, such as the advance-decline ratio, can complement sentiment analysis.

If sentiment is excessively bullish, but market breadth is weakening, it may signal an impending correction.

4. Economic Indicators: Economic data can provide additional context. Contrarian investors often consider macroeconomic indicators when evaluating sentiment. If sentiment is overwhelmingly bearish, but economic data suggests improving conditions, it could signal a contrarian opportunity.


**Building a Sentiment-Based Investment Strategy**
Now that we've filtered out the noise and combined sentiment with other indicators, it's time to construct a sentiment-based investment strategy. A robust strategy should incorporate the following elements:

1. Sentiment Thresholds: Define specific sentiment thresholds that trigger action. For instance, you may decide to buy when sentiment falls below a certain level and sell when it reaches an extreme high. These thresholds act as your guideposts in the noisy world of sentiment analysis.

2. Contrarian Signals: Develop a set of contrarian signals based on sentiment and other indicators. These signals should dictate when to enter or exit a position. For example, a contrarian buy signal could occur when sentiment is excessively bearish, and technical indicators confirm an oversold condition.

3. Portfolio Allocation: Determine how much of your portfolio you are willing to allocate to sentiment-driven

investments. This allocation should align with your risk tolerance and overall portfolio strategy.

4. Continuous Monitoring: Sentiment is dynamic, and so should be your strategy. Regularly monitor sentiment data, adjust your thresholds if necessary, and be prepared to act swiftly when contrarian signals are triggered.

5. Risk Management: Always incorporate risk management techniques into your sentiment-based strategy. Set stop-loss levels, diversify your investments, and ensure your overall portfolio remains balanced.

In the field of contrarian investing, sentiment analysis is a potent partner. By critically analyzing sentiment data, combining it with other indicators, and building a well-defined strategy, you equip yourself to navigate the noise and uncover the true signals that can lead to profitable contrarian moves. Remember, the key is to remain disciplined and unswayed by the crowd's emotional rollercoaster, focusing instead on the rational analysis of sentiment-driven opportunities.

# Chapter 4: Contrarian Strategies in Different Asset Classes

## 4.1 Contrarian Investing in Stocks

Stocks have long been the focal point of contrarian investing. The equity markets, with their volatile nature and propensity for herding behavior, offer a fertile ground for contrarians to seek out opportunities that others may overlook. In this subchapter, we will delve into the intricacies of contrarian investing in stocks, exploring stock screening techniques, the art of building a diversified stock portfolio, and effective risk management strategies.

### Stock Screening Techniques: The Art of Selecting Diamonds in the Rough

Contrarian investors do not randomly select stocks to add to their portfolios; they employ a systematic approach that involves thorough research and screening techniques to identify potential candidates for investment. It's akin to a prospector sifting through gravel to uncover precious gems. Here are some key methods contrarians use to screen stocks:

1. Price-to-Earnings (P/E) Ratio: The P/E ratio is a fundamental metric that compares a stock's current market price to its earnings per share. Contrarians often seek stocks with low P/E ratios, as they may be undervalued compared to their peers. However, a low P/E ratio alone is not sufficient; contrarians also assess whether the low valuation is justified by fundamental factors.

2. Price-to-Book (P/B) Ratio: A low P/B ratio suggests that a stock may be trading below its book value, indicating potential undervaluation. Contrarians look for stocks with low P/B ratios relative to historical averages and industry peers.

3. Price-to-Sales (P/S) Ratio: The P/S ratio measures a stock's price relative to its revenue. A low P/S ratio can indicate that a stock is undervalued, but it requires further analysis to confirm. Contrarians assess whether the ratio aligns with the stock's industry and historical norms.

4. Contrarian Indicators: Contrarians have a unique toolkit of specialized indicators that help them identify overbought or oversold conditions. For instance, they might use the Relative Strength Index (RSI) or the McClellan Oscillator to gauge market sentiment and identify potential contrarian opportunities.

5. Earnings Growth: Contrarians look for stocks with solid earnings growth potential, especially if the market sentiment has turned negative on the company. They assess whether there is a divergence between the stock's price and its expected earnings growth.

6. Dividend Yield: High dividend yields can be attractive to contrarians, particularly if they believe the market has unfairly discounted the stock due to short-term challenges. Contrarians assess whether the dividend is sustainable and whether there's potential for dividend growth.

7. Contrarian News Screening: Contrarians actively seek out news that has led to negative market sentiment. They

scrutinize news for possible overreactions and assess whether underlying fundamentals are intact. It's not about avoiding bad news but deciphering its true impact.

It's important to note that contrarian stock screening is not solely about finding the lowest-priced stocks. Rather, it involves a comprehensive evaluation of a stock's fundamentals and its potential for a price correction. Contrarians understand that low prices alone do not guarantee success; they must be supported by solid underlying value.

## Building a Diversified Stock Portfolio: Balancing Risk and Reward

Contrarians understand that successful investing is not about putting all your eggs in one basket but rather skillfully diversifying across multiple assets. The art of building a diversified stock portfolio is a delicate balancing act that involves the following considerations:

1. Sector Diversification: Contrarians spread their investments across different sectors of the economy. This approach helps reduce exposure to sector-specific risks. For example, if one sector is facing headwinds, investments in other sectors may offset potential losses.

2. Market Capitalization: Contrarians consider stocks of varying market capitalizations. They may hold positions in large-cap, mid-cap, and small-cap stocks to capture opportunities across the spectrum. Different-sized companies may react differently to market conditions.

3. Geographic Diversification: Global diversification can help contrarians navigate regional economic fluctuations. By investing in stocks from different geographic regions, they reduce the impact of adverse regional events.

4. Asset Classes: Contrarians may also diversify by including other asset classes, such as bonds, real estate investment trusts (REITs), or alternative investments, to add balance to their portfolios. Diversifying across asset classes can help hedge against market volatility.

5. Position Sizing: Contrarians allocate capital to individual stocks based on their risk tolerance and confidence in the contrarian thesis. They may allocate larger positions to stocks they believe have a higher contrarian potential.

6. Regular Rebalancing: Contrarians periodically review and rebalance their portfolios to ensure that their diversification remains intact. Rebalancing involves adjusting positions based on changing market conditions. If one sector has outperformed others, rebalancing may involve trimming positions in that sector and adding to underperforming sectors to maintain desired allocations.

Diversification is not just a risk management technique for contrarians; it's a strategic approach that allows them to capture contrarian opportunities while spreading risk. By diversifying across different sectors, market capitalizations, and geographic regions, contrarians aim to build resilient portfolios that can weather market turbulence.

**Managing Risk in Stock Investing: Navigating the Seas of Uncertainty**

Effective risk management is the cornerstone of successful contrarian stock investing. Contrarians understand that the path to profits is not always smooth, and markets can be turbulent waters. They employ several strategies to manage risk:

1. Stop-Loss Orders: Contrarians often set stop-loss orders to limit potential losses. These orders automatically trigger a sale if a stock's price reaches a predetermined level, helping to contain losses. Stop-loss orders are a crucial tool to prevent small losses from turning into significant ones.

2. Position Sizing: Contrarians carefully determine the size of each position in their portfolio. By sizing positions appropriately, they control the impact of individual stock movements on their overall portfolio. This approach prevents overexposure to high-risk assets.

3. Diversification: As mentioned earlier, diversification is a fundamental risk management strategy. By spreading investments across different stocks and sectors, contrarians reduce the impact of poor performance in a single asset.

4. Risk Assessment: Contrarians assess the risk-reward ratio for each investment. They weigh the potential upside against the downside risk and avoid investments where the potential loss outweighs the potential gain. Prudent risk assessment guides their investment decisions.

5. Continuous Monitoring: Contrarians regularly monitor their portfolio and the broader market. They remain vigilant

for any changes in the contrarian thesis or signs that may necessitate adjustments to their positions. Continuous monitoring helps them adapt to changing market conditions.

6. Patience: Contrarians understand that not all contrarian investments will yield immediate results. They exhibit patience, allowing their contrarian theses to play out over time. Impatience can lead to premature exits and missed opportunities.

7. Stress Testing: Contrarians stress test their portfolios to assess how they may perform under adverse conditions. This involves simulating scenarios in which the market moves against their contrarian positions. Stress testing helps them gauge the resilience of their portfolio and identify potential weaknesses.

Contrarian investing in stocks is a disciplined and systematic approach. It involves careful screening, diversification, and vigilant risk management. By adhering to these principles, contrarians position themselves to seize opportunities in the stock market and navigate its inherent volatility with confidence. Remember, in the realm of contrarian investing, knowledge and preparation are your allies in the quest for financial success.

## 4.2 Contrarian Approaches to Bonds and Fixed Income

In the vast landscape of contrarian investing, stocks often take center stage as the focal point of attention. Yet, within the world of investments, bonds and fixed income instruments provide an entirely distinct arena for contrarian strategies to shine. Contrarian approaches to bonds and fixed income can be just as rewarding, if not more so, for those who understand their nuances. In this subchapter, we will explore the unique dynamics of fixed income markets, uncover the contrarian opportunities they present, delve into the factors that shape these markets, and unveil yield curve strategies that can bolster your contrarian bond investments.

### Bond Market Contrarian Opportunities

While equities tend to capture the limelight when it comes to contrarian investing, fixed income markets offer a treasure trove of contrarian opportunities for astute investors. Contrarians in this realm look for instances where the prevailing market sentiment has driven bond prices to extremes, creating opportunities for contrarian plays. Here are some common contrarian opportunities within the bond market:

1. Overlooked or Undervalued Bonds: Contrarian bond investors seek out bonds that have been overlooked or undervalued due to negative sentiment or market turmoil. These can include corporate bonds of companies facing

temporary setbacks or government bonds from countries perceived as risky.

2. High-Yield Bonds (Junk Bonds): When fear grips the market, high-yield bonds often face heightened selling pressure, causing their prices to drop. Contrarian investors may step in when these bonds become oversold, seizing the opportunity to capture high yields at discounted prices.

3. Municipal Bonds: Municipal bonds, issued by state and local governments, can be subject to market sentiment swings. Contrarians might look for instances where negative news, such as a local economic downturn or fiscal challenges, have created attractive entry points into municipal bond markets.

4. Contrarian Interest Rate Plays: As interest rates rise, bond prices tend to fall, and vice versa. Contrarian bond investors assess whether prevailing interest rate expectations are overblown. When they believe the market has overly discounted future rate increases, they may take contrarian positions by buying bonds, expecting rates to stabilize or even decline.

## Factors Affecting Fixed Income Markets

To excel in contrarian fixed income investing, one must grasp the factors that exert influence over these markets. While equity markets often respond to company-specific news and economic indicators, fixed income markets have their unique set of drivers:

1. Interest Rates: Interest rates, controlled by central banks, play a pivotal role in fixed income markets. Contrarian bond investors closely monitor interest rate movements and assess whether market expectations are overreacting to potential rate changes.

2. Credit Quality: The creditworthiness of bond issuers is a critical factor. Contrarian investors scrutinize credit ratings and may identify opportunities when market pessimism about an issuer's creditworthiness is exaggerated.

3. Inflation: Inflation erodes the purchasing power of fixed income investments. Contrarian bond investors consider whether inflation fears are overdone or underestimated, as this can impact bond prices and yields.

4. Economic Conditions: Contrarian fixed income strategies take into account broader economic conditions. They look for situations where market sentiment about economic trends is excessively pessimistic or optimistic.

5. Political and Geopolitical Events: Events such as elections, geopolitical tensions, or government policy changes can impact fixed income markets. Contrarians assess whether market reactions to these events are rational or exaggerated.

**Yield Curve Strategies**
The yield curve is a graphical representation of interest rates for bonds of varying maturities. Contrarian bond investors leverage insights from the yield curve to

formulate their strategies. Here are key yield curve strategies in contrarian bond investing:

**Figure 2 (US Bonds 10 Year Yields slowly rise in 2022)**

1. Steepening Yield Curve: A steepening yield curve occurs when long-term interest rates rise relative to short-term rates. Contrarian investors may view this as an opportunity to purchase long-term bonds, expecting their prices to appreciate as rates stabilize.

2. Flattening Yield Curve: A flattening yield curve is the opposite, with long-term rates falling relative to short-term rates. Contrarians may consider shortening their bond maturities during a flattening curve phase, anticipating potential future rate increases.

3. Inverted Yield Curve: An inverted yield curve arises when short-term rates surpass long-term rates. Contrarian bond investors watch for this as an indicator of potential economic downturns. They might favor short-term bonds or

other safe-haven assets in anticipation of market turbulence.

4. Normalizing Yield Curve: Contrarians pay attention to shifts in the yield curve toward a more normal state. They analyze whether the curve is reverting to a historical average, potentially creating opportunities in the process.

Mastering these strategies and understanding the foundation of factors that influence fixed income markets is essential. Contrarian bond investors navigate through market sentiment, applying contrarian wisdom to identify undervalued opportunities that the crowd may overlook. Whether it's seizing the moment during a yield curve inversion or recognizing the value hidden in high-yield bonds, contrarian approaches to bonds and fixed income can be a compelling addition to your investment toolkit.

## 4.3 Contrarian Tactics in Real Estate and Alternative Investments

Real estate and alternative investments form a distinctive realm within the universe of contrarian investing. They offer an enticing departure from the more conventional stocks and bonds, bestowing upon astute contrarian investors the potential to diversify their portfolios and uncover opportunities often eluding the notice of mainstream market participants. In this subchapter, we'll delve into the critical aspects of timing your contrarian moves, understanding market cycles, utilizing essential tools, and managing risks along the way.

**Real Estate as a Contrarian Asset**

Real estate, the bastion of wealth-building for generations, presents an intriguing landscape for contrarian investors. Rather than viewing real estate as a monolithic entity, contrarians scrutinize it with a discerning eye, recognizing that market sentiment can oscillate from euphoria to despondency, paving the way for distinctive contrarian opportunities.

1. Market Cycles in Real Estate: Paralleling the stock and bond markets, the real estate sector traverses discernible cycles. During the exuberant phases of a real estate boom, property prices may ascend to seemingly unsustainable heights, invariably enticing investors to join the fervor. Contrarians, however, exhibit prudence and circumspection, reserving their judgment as they await telltale signs of overvaluation. Conversely, when the pendulum of market sentiment swings towards pessimism, heralding the advent of a downturn, contrarians seize upon the ensuing market despondency to acquire properties at prices distinctly discounted from their intrinsic worth.

2. Counter-Cyclical Investing: A hallmark of contrarian real estate investing is the adoption of a counter-cyclical stance. Contrarians eschew the herd mentality that typically prevails in the real estate sector and act against prevailing market trends. For instance, during a housing bubble, when

the allure of exorbitant property prices can prove irresistible to many, contrarians exhibit restraint, choosing instead to diversify their real estate holdings or explore alternative markets that offer more enticing valuations.

3. Distressed Properties: Contrarian investors are often magnetically drawn to distressed properties, an area ripe with contrarian potential. Distressed properties encompass a spectrum that includes foreclosures, short sales, and properties in dire need of extensive rehabilitation. These assets are typically found languishing in the shadows, overlooked by the broader market due to their perceived risk and challenges. Yet, for the discerning contrarian, these properties represent opportunities replete with the potential for substantial appreciation if adeptly managed.

**Exploring Alternative Investment Opportunities**
Beyond the realm of traditional real estate holdings, contrarian investors boldly venture into a kaleidoscope of alternative investments, each offering a unique and tantalizing contrarian allure. These alternative assets form an eclectic ensemble, presenting a diversified palette of opportunities for those with the acumen to discern their potential.

1. Precious Metals: Precious metals such as gold and silver stand as bedrock assets in the contrarian's portfolio. These metals are often viewed as hedges against economic uncertainty and inflation. When conventional investments falter and market confidence erodes, the intrinsic value of

precious metals has historically demonstrated the capacity to surge.

2. Collectibles: The world of collectibles, including rare coins, vintage stamps, fine art, and vintage automobiles, holds particular fascination for contrarian investors. These tangible assets, often regarded as items of passion, can also serve as alternative investments. Contrarians engage in meticulous research to uncover niches within the collectibles market that exhibit the potential for appreciable gains.

3. Private Equity and Venture Capital: The realm of private equity and venture capital is another arena where contrarians find themselves at home. Investing in privately held companies or startups can be a bold contrarian move. While these investments inherently entail elevated risk levels, they possess the potential to yield substantial returns if discerningly selected.

4. Commodities: Contrarian investors explore the world of commodities, encompassing resources such as oil, natural gas, and agricultural products. These assets often exhibit pronounced price volatility and can be susceptible to shifts in market sentiment. Contrarians discern opportunities when prices languish at troughs, reflecting bearish sentiment and market disfavor.


**Combining Asset Classes for a Balanced Portfolio**
Contrarian investors, as architects of their financial destinies, bear the responsibility of fashioning portfolios

that are resilient and diversified. The careful interplay between traditional investments like stocks and bonds and the more eclectic realm of alternative assets forms the cornerstone of their portfolio management strategy.

1. Asset Allocation: Contrarian investors are distinguished by their meticulous approach to asset allocation. Their choices are deeply informed by their contrarian outlook for each asset class. For instance, in periods of rampant exuberance within the stock market, contrarians may opt to reduce their exposure to overvalued equities while concurrently bolstering their allocations to undervalued real estate or alternative investments.

2. Correlation Considerations: An integral facet of contrarian portfolio construction revolves around the assessment of correlations between asset classes. The astute contrarian recognizes that assets exhibiting inverse price movements can serve as effective hedges, insulating portfolios against catastrophic losses in one sector.

3. Risk Mitigation: The inclusion of alternative investments within portfolios represents a potent means of mitigating risk. These assets often exhibit low or even negative correlations with traditional investments, thereby conferring upon portfolios an added layer of protection during turbulent market phases.

4. Long-Term Perspective: Contrarian investors are attuned to the extended investment horizons frequently associated with alternative assets. They embrace the mantle of patience, cognizant that the appreciation of alternative

investments may unfurl over protracted timeframes, all the while diligently monitoring their contrarian indicators.

5. Portfolio Rebalancing: Regular portfolio rebalancing stands as an indispensable facet of contrarian portfolio management. It affords investors the capacity to assess the performance of each asset class and, in accordance with their contrarian perspective, recalibrate their allocations to uphold their desired risk-reward equilibrium.

The deployment of contrarian tactics within the realms of real estate and alternative investments bequeaths investors with an expansive repertoire of strategies to diversify their portfolios and to seize opportunities that would otherwise remain obscured. Contrarian investors perceive these asset classes not as deviations from the norm but as fertile terrains for unearthing latent value. Whether it be the sagacious timing of real estate acquisitions within cyclical markets or the exploration of alternative assets during epochs of financial turbulence, the indomitable contrarian mindset emerges as a beacon of opportunity in the constantly evolving landscape of investments.

# Chapter 5: Implementing Your Contrarian Investment Plan

## 5.1 Creating a Personalized Investment Plan

Contrarian investing is not a one-size-fits-all strategy. The effectiveness of your contrarian approach hinges on your ability to create a personalized investment plan that aligns with your unique financial goals, risk tolerance, and timeline. In this subchapter, we will explore the critical steps involved in crafting a personalized contrarian investment plan that can guide you on your path to financial success.

### Tailoring Strategies to Your Goals

The foundation of any successful contrarian investment plan is a clear understanding of your financial objectives. Contrarian strategies can be diverse, ranging from value-based stock picking to contrarian macroeconomic plays. The key is to align your chosen strategies with your unique goals:

1. Short-Term vs. Long-Term Objectives: Start by defining your investment horizon. Are you seeking short-term gains, such as funding a vacation or a down payment on a home? Or are you focused on long-term wealth accumulation, like retirement or generational wealth? Your timeframe will dictate the strategies you employ.

2. Risk Tolerance Assessment: Contrarian investing can be inherently riskier than more conventional approaches. Assess your risk tolerance honestly. How comfortable are

you with the possibility of short-term volatility in pursuit of potentially higher returns? Understanding your risk tolerance will help you shape your investment plan.

3. Income Generation vs. Capital Appreciation: Contrarian strategies can also vary in terms of generating income versus seeking capital appreciation. Are you looking for regular income to cover living expenses, or are you aiming for growth in asset value over time? Your choice will influence the assets you select.

4. Sector and Asset Class Preferences: Consider your sector and asset class preferences. Are you particularly interested in contrarian opportunities in technology stocks, real estate, or perhaps commodities? Tailor your contrarian approach to focus on areas of the market that align with your interests and expertise.

5. Sustainable vs. Aggressive Growth: Some contrarian investors opt for sustainable growth, targeting assets with long-term potential and stability. Others may be more inclined towards aggressive growth, taking calculated risks in pursuit of substantial gains. Determine your growth preferences.

**Setting Specific Investment Rules**
Contrarian investing requires a disciplined approach. It's not about making impulsive decisions based on gut feelings. To maintain consistency and navigate the contrarian path effectively, establish specific investment rules:

1. Entry and Exit Criteria: Define clear criteria for when to enter and exit investments. This could involve using technical indicators, fundamental thresholds, or sentiment metrics. Having predefined rules ensures you're not swayed by emotions.

2. Position Sizing Guidelines: Determine the maximum percentage of your portfolio that you'll allocate to a single contrarian investment. This prevents overexposure to any one asset and mitigates risk.

3. Risk Management Rules: Establish rules for managing risk. For instance, specify the maximum percentage of your portfolio that you're willing to risk on a single contrarian position. Additionally, outline strategies for dealing with unexpected market developments.

4. Monitoring and Review Schedule: Set a regular schedule for reviewing your portfolio and making adjustments. This might be quarterly, semi-annually, or annually. Regular assessments help ensure your investments stay aligned with your goals.

5. Contingency Plans: Consider scenarios where your contrarian investments do not go as planned. What will you do if an asset faces prolonged declines? Having contingency plans in place can prevent impulsive decisions during difficult times.

**Portfolio Rebalancing Strategies**
Successful contrarian investors recognize that the market is dynamic, and asset values are constantly shifting. To

maintain a balanced and effective portfolio, you must implement robust rebalancing strategies. Here's how to go about it:

1. Regular Monitoring: Keep a close eye on your portfolio's performance and the market's overall trajectory. Regular monitoring ensures that you're aware of any significant changes that may require action.

2. Threshold-Based Rebalancing: Establish threshold percentages for each asset class in your portfolio. When an asset's weight deviates from its target by a predetermined percentage, rebalance by buying or selling to restore the desired allocation.

3. Periodic Rebalancing: Alternatively, you can rebalance your portfolio at regular intervals, such as quarterly or annually. This approach simplifies the process and helps maintain consistency.

4. Tax-Efficient Rebalancing: Consider the tax implications of rebalancing. In taxable accounts, focus on minimizing capital gains taxes by selling assets with lower gains or losses.

5. Review and Adjust: Periodically review your investment rules and goals to ensure they remain aligned with your financial situation and objectives. Adjust your personalized investment plan as needed.

6. Embrace Contrarian Opportunities: Be open to contrarian opportunities that may arise during rebalancing. If an asset class becomes undervalued or overvalued due to market sentiment, consider adjusting your allocation accordingly.

Creating a personalized contrarian investment plan is the cornerstone of your journey toward financial success. It ensures that your contrarian strategies align with your unique goals, risk tolerance, and time horizon. By setting specific investment rules and implementing disciplined portfolio rebalancing strategies, you'll navigate the ups and downs of the market with confidence and purpose.

Remember that contrarian investing is not a static endeavor; it's a dynamic journey that adapts to your evolving circumstances and market conditions. Your personalized investment plan should serve as a flexible guide that helps you navigate the ever-changing investment landscape while staying true to your contrarian principles.

## 5.2 Evaluating Your Contrarian Investments

Your journey into the world of contrarian investing has been marked by careful analysis, calculated risks, and strategic decision-making. But the journey doesn't end with the purchase of undervalued assets. Successful contrarian investors know that evaluating and managing their investments is a continuous process—one that involves monitoring performance, making adjustments, and navigating tax considerations. In this subchapter, we'll explore these critical aspects to ensure that your contrarian investment plan remains on course.

## Monitoring Performance Metrics

Effective evaluation of your contrarian investments begins with a deep understanding of performance metrics. These metrics serve as the compass guiding your investment decisions and helping you measure the success of your contrarian strategies. Here are some key performance metrics contrarian investors routinely employ:

1. Total Return: Total return assesses the overall performance of your investment, accounting for both capital appreciation (or depreciation) and any income generated from dividends or interest. Contrarians track total return to gauge the profitability of their investments.

2. Alpha: Alpha measures the excess return of an investment compared to its benchmark index. A positive alpha suggests that the investment outperformed the benchmark, indicating successful contrarian decision-making.

3. Beta: Beta quantifies an investment's sensitivity to market movements. Contrarian investors often seek assets with low beta values, indicating lower volatility and potentially smoother contrarian rides during market turbulence.

4. Sharpe Ratio: The Sharpe ratio assesses an investment's risk-adjusted return. Contrarians aim for a high Sharpe ratio, indicating that their investments provide a superior return relative to the level of risk undertaken.

5. Win-Loss Ratio: Contrarians keep track of their investment wins and losses to understand their success rate.

While contrarian investing doesn't guarantee every investment will be a winner, a favorable win-loss ratio indicates effective contrarian strategies.

6. Drawdown: Drawdown measures the peak-to-trough decline in an investment's value. Contrarians are vigilant in monitoring drawdown to ensure that losses are controlled and within acceptable limits.

7. Tracking Error: Tracking error quantifies how closely an investment follows its benchmark index. Contrarians may use tracking error to assess whether their portfolios deviate significantly from their intended contrarian strategies.

## Adjusting Your Portfolio Over Time

Contrarian investing is not a "set it and forget it" approach. As market conditions change and new information emerges, it's essential to make adjustments to your portfolio. Here's a strategic framework for adapting your contrarian investments over time:

1. Regular Review: Set a schedule for reviewing your portfolio. Contrarian investors often perform quarterly or annual assessments. During these reviews, analyze the performance metrics mentioned earlier.

2. Rebalancing: Rebalancing involves adjusting your portfolio to maintain your desired asset allocation. If certain assets have appreciated significantly and now represent a larger portion of your portfolio than intended, consider selling some of them and reallocating the proceeds

to assets that may have underperformed but remain undervalued.

3. Asset Selection: Continuously evaluate the assets in your portfolio. Are they still undervalued, or has their contrarian potential diminished? Be prepared to sell assets that no longer align with your contrarian strategy and replace them with new opportunities.

4. Risk Management: As your portfolio grows or market conditions change, your risk profile may shift. Adjust your risk management strategies accordingly. For example, if you've experienced substantial gains, consider implementing trailing stop-loss orders to protect your profits.

5. Stay Informed: Keep a close watch on economic and market developments. Contrarian investing is based on contrarian indicators and market inefficiencies. Being aware of changing market sentiment and conditions is crucial for effective decision-making.

**Tax Considerations for Contrarian Investors**
Taxes are an essential aspect of investing, and contrarian investors must be mindful of their tax obligations. Proper tax planning can help you maximize your after-tax returns and ensure that your contrarian profits remain intact. Here are some tax considerations for contrarian investors:

1. Capital Gains Tax: When you sell an investment for a profit, you may incur capital gains tax. Contrarian investors should be aware of tax rates and exemptions related to

long-term and short-term gains. Consider holding assets for the long term to benefit from lower tax rates on long-term gains.

2. Tax-Efficient Accounts: Utilize tax-efficient accounts such as Individual Retirement Accounts (IRAs) and 401(k)s to shield your contrarian investments from immediate taxation. These accounts offer tax advantages, such as tax-deferred growth or tax-free withdrawals in retirement.

3. Tax-Loss Harvesting: Contrarian investors can strategically use tax-loss harvesting to offset capital gains with capital losses. By selling underperforming assets at a loss, you can reduce your tax liability.

4. Asset Location: Consider the tax efficiency of your investments and allocate them strategically across taxable and tax-advantaged accounts. Assets with higher tax burdens, such as bonds with interest income, are often better placed in tax-advantaged accounts.

5. Estate Planning: Effective estate planning can help you minimize the tax impact on your heirs. Consider gifting appreciated assets, establishing trusts, or utilizing other estate planning strategies to preserve your contrarian wealth.

6. Consult a Tax Professional: Tax laws are complex and subject to change. It's advisable to consult a tax professional or financial advisor who specializes in tax-efficient investing to navigate the intricacies of tax planning effectively.

Evaluating your contrarian investments, making necessary adjustments, and considering tax implications are integral to your long-term success as a contrarian investor. By mastering these aspects, you'll not only protect and grow your wealth but also optimize your contrarian strategy for the ever-changing financial landscape. Contrarian investing is a journey that demands vigilance, adaptability, and a commitment to financial excellence, and you are well on your way to achieving it.

## 5.3 Common Pitfalls and How to Avoid Them

Contrarian investing, while a powerful strategy, is not without its challenges. The path to contrarian success is riddled with potential pitfalls that can derail even the most well-informed and disciplined investors. In this subchapter, we'll explore these common pitfalls and, more importantly, how to navigate them successfully.

### Recognizing Cognitive Biases

One of the most formidable foes a contrarian investor faces is their own mind. The human brain is wired with cognitive biases—systematic patterns of deviation from rationality— that can cloud judgment and lead to poor investment decisions. Recognizing and mitigating these biases is essential for success.

Confirmation Bias: This bias leads us to seek out information that confirms our existing beliefs while ignoring or dismissing contradictory evidence. In contrarian investing, this can manifest as the tendency to only see what aligns with our contrarian thesis while disregarding warning signs.

Overconfidence Bias: Overconfidence can lead investors to overestimate their knowledge and abilities, causing them to take excessive risks. Contrarians should remain humble and acknowledge the limits of their knowledge.

Anchoring Bias: Anchoring occurs when investors fixate on a specific price or value, often the purchase price of an asset. Contrarians must be willing to reevaluate their positions based on changing information rather than anchoring to past decisions.

Herd Mentality: Even contrarians can fall prey to herd mentality, particularly during moments of extreme market stress. The fear of missing out or the desire to conform to the majority can lead to irrational decisions.

**Staying Disciplined in Contrarian Investing**
Contrarian investing demands a high degree of discipline. The allure of following the crowd or succumbing to emotional reactions can be strong. Staying disciplined in your contrarian approach requires several key strategies:

Establish Clear Investment Rules: Before embarking on your contrarian journey, define clear rules for your investment strategy. Determine criteria for asset selection, entry, and exit points. Having a well-defined plan helps you avoid impulsive decisions.

Stick to Your Research: The foundation of contrarian investing is rigorous research and analysis. Once you've done your due diligence, stick to your convictions. Avoid the temptation to second-guess yourself based on short-term market fluctuations.

Set Realistic Expectations: Contrarian investing doesn't guarantee instant success. Acknowledge that contrarian moves may take time to play out. Set realistic expectations for your investments and avoid the lure of quick riches.

Avoid Chasing Trends: Contrarian investors must resist the urge to chase the latest trends or follow the crowd. Stay true to your contrarian principles, even when it seems like the market is moving in the opposite direction.

Monitor Your Emotions: Emotional reactions can be the downfall of contrarian investors. Fear and greed can cloud judgment and lead to impulsive decisions. Regularly assess your emotional state and take a step back when necessary.

## Preparing for Market Volatility

Contrarian investing often involves navigating choppy waters, and market volatility is the norm rather than the exception. To thrive in this environment, it's crucial to be prepared for market turbulence:

Diversify Your Portfolio: While contrarian investing focuses on individual assets, a diversified portfolio can help mitigate the impact of market volatility. By holding a variety of assets, you spread risk and reduce vulnerability to market swings.

Maintain a Cash Cushion: Having cash reserves at your disposal can provide peace of mind during volatile times. Cash allows you to take advantage of contrarian opportunities when others may be forced to sell at unfavorable prices.

Use Stop-Loss Orders Wisely: Stop-loss orders can protect your capital in volatile markets. However, set them carefully to avoid being prematurely stopped out due to short-term price fluctuations.

Stay Informed and Adaptive: Market conditions change, and contrarian opportunities evolve. Stay informed about economic developments, news, and trends that could impact your investments. Be ready to adapt your strategy as circumstances change.

Keep a Long-Term Perspective: Short-term volatility is a given in the world of contrarian investing. Maintain a long-term perspective and remember that your investment thesis may take time to materialize.

In the field of contrarian investing, recognizing and mitigating cognitive biases, staying disciplined, and preparing for market volatility are essential steps on the path to success. By mastering these aspects, you position yourself to navigate the challenges that come your way and harness the power of contrarian thinking to build a resilient and profitable investment portfolio.

# Chapter 6: Case Studies in Contrarian Investing

## Case Study 1 - The Contrarian Legends

In the annals of financial history, there are few names as revered and influential as Benjamin Graham and Warren Buffett. These two individuals, separated by a generation but united by their contrarian investment philosophies, have left an indelible mark on the world of finance. Their stories are not just tales of wealth accumulation; they are narratives of resilience, unwavering discipline, and an unrelenting commitment to contrarian principles.

Benjamin Graham, often referred to as the "Father of Value Investing," laid the groundwork for contrarian investing as we know it today. His magnum opus, "Security Analysis," written during the aftermath of the Great Depression, outlined the principles of value investing with an emphasis on risk mitigation. Graham's concept of the "margin of safety" became a cornerstone of contrarian thought. He believed that investors should purchase assets at prices significantly below their intrinsic value, thus insulating themselves from market volatility and irrational exuberance. Graham's contrarian discipline was unwavering; he advocated a meticulous analysis of financial statements, a steadfast adherence to fundamental analysis, and a deep-rooted skepticism of market sentiment. Perhaps his most enduring lesson was the idea that market crises were not to be feared but embraced, as they presented opportunities to buy sound businesses at substantial discounts.

Warren Buffett, often heralded as one of the greatest investors of all time, is a testament to the enduring power of contrarian principles. Buffett was a student of Graham's at Columbia Business School, and the lessons he learned from his mentor shaped his investment philosophy. One of the key takeaways from Graham was the idea that contrarianism was not merely about buying distressed assets; it was also about recognizing value where others did not. Buffett's focus on quality, a departure from the conventional contrarian playbook, underlines his belief that contrarianism could mean investing in strong, well-managed businesses trading at discounts. His contrarian approach is marked by patience—a willingness to hold investments indefinitely, regardless of short-term market fluctuations. This long-term vision is quintessential contrarianism, as it requires unwavering conviction and the ability to tune out the noise of market sentiment. Buffett's enduring success is a testament to his contrarian independence of thought, as he charted his own course based on a rigorous analysis of intrinsic value.

The lessons we derive from these contrarian legends are far-reaching. They remind us that the heart of contrarian investing lies in the pursuit of value, whether through distressed assets or undervalued quality companies. Discipline is the bedrock of contrarian success, requiring meticulous analysis, prudent decision-making, and the resolve to remain resolute when others waver. Patience, another critical trait, is the contrarian's ally, allowing them to weather market turbulence and reap the rewards of long-term conviction. Independence of thought, a hallmark of both Graham and Buffett, underscores the importance of thinking differently and resisting the herd mentality. Lastly, these contrarian luminaries were lifelong learners, constantly adapting their strategies and remaining open to new ideas—a lesson that applies equally to modern contrarian investors.

The legends of contrarian investing, Benjamin Graham and Warren Buffett, leave us with a treasury of timeless lessons. They extol the primacy of value, the necessity of discipline, and the rewards of patience. They remind us that contrarianism is not the pursuit of quick gains but the patient cultivation of enduring wealth. Their narratives are hymns to independent thought and lifelong learning, urging contrarians to remain vigilant in a world where conformity often overshadows contrarian wisdom. As we continue our exploration into the realm of contrarian investing, let us carry forward the torch lit by these giants, using their stories as compasses to navigate the ever-shifting tides of financial markets.

## Case Study 2 - The Dot-Com Bubble and Its Contrarians

At the turn of the 21st century, the financial world witnessed the breathtaking rise and catastrophic fall of the Dot-Com Bubble, a period marked by fervent speculation in internet-based companies. As stock prices soared to astronomical levels, traditional valuation metrics seemed to be tossed aside, and investors rushed to buy into anything bearing the ".com" label. Yet, within this maelstrom of irrational exuberance, a cadre of astute contrarian investors stood as sentinels of caution, recognizing that what goes up must eventually come down.

Among these contrarians was the sage of Omaha himself, Warren Buffett. While not typically associated with the technology sector, Buffett voiced his concerns in his 1999 letter to Berkshire Hathaway shareholders. In his characteristic plainspoken manner, he warned against the reckless optimism that had taken hold, likening it to a Pied Piper leading investors down a treacherous path. His message was clear and unwavering: the fundamentals of investing still held true, and valuations could not be ignored.

Another contrarian luminary, Stanley Druckenmiller, took a more proactive approach. He chose to short technology stocks, effectively betting against the prevailing euphoria. Druckenmiller's contrarian stance was grounded in the belief that the market had departed from rationality, that it had become a realm where speculation eclipsed sound judgment. His early warnings and decisive actions, as we would later see, would prove to be nothing short of prescient.

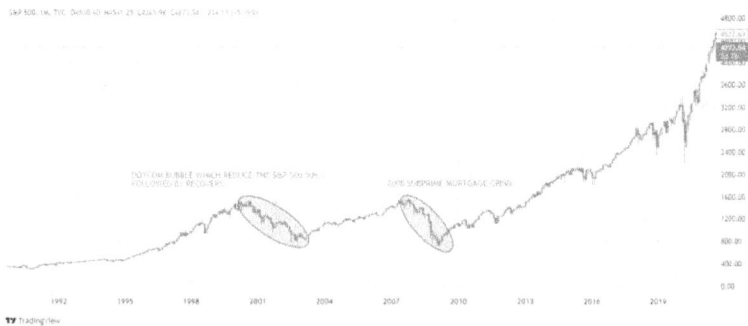

**Figure 3 (2000 dot com bubble market decline followed by rebound in and 2008 crisis followed by rise in S&P 500)**

As the Dot-Com Bubble inflated to ever more perilous proportions, contrarian investors adopted a series of calculated strategies to shield their portfolios from the impending storm. They began by reducing their exposure to technology stocks, recognizing that valuations had stretched to unsustainable levels. Short selling became a key instrument in their toolkit, allowing them to profit from the inevitable correction as they bet against overpriced stocks. Throughout this period, contrarians remained resolute in their adherence to fundamental analysis, focusing on companies with solid financials, reasonable valuations, and a clear path to profitability. Some sought refuge in more conservative sectors like consumer staples and utilities, industries known for their resilience in the face of market volatility.

When the Dot-Com Bubble finally burst in 2000, it sent shockwaves through financial markets, inflicting substantial losses on many investors. Yet, amidst the wreckage, contrarian investors saw a new landscape, ripe with opportunities. The technology sector lay in ruins, with stock prices of once high-flying companies reduced to mere fractions of their former glory. It was a value hunter's paradise. Contrarians carefully sifted through the debris, seeking out hidden gems among the ruins—companies with solid fundamentals that had been unjustly punished by the market's indiscriminate wrath.

Beyond value hunting, contrarian investors also saw opportunities in rebalancing their portfolios. They trimmed positions in sectors that had inflated during the bubble and redirected capital toward undervalued segments of the market. Those who had accurately identified survivors from the wreckage found themselves in a prime position to invest in companies with genuine potential, now trading at attractive valuations.

One investor who exemplified this post-bubble contrarian success was David Tepper. His Appaloosa Management made bold investments in distressed technology stocks, including Micron Technology and Nortel Networks. These investments would go on to deliver substantial returns, a testament to the foresight and courage of contrarian investors.

The Dot-Com Bubble remains an indelible chapter in the history of financial markets, serving as a vivid reminder of the perils of speculative excess. It also stands as a testament to the resilience and wisdom of contrarian investors who, by adhering to time-honored principles of valuation and prudence, not only weathered the storm but emerged stronger and more prosperous on the other side. In the world of contrarian investing, it is a vivid illustration of the enduring power of foresight and discipline, even when surrounded by irrational exuberance.

## Case Study 3 - Recent Contrarian Triumphs

Contrarian investing is not a relic of the past; it's a living, evolving strategy that continues to find success in the modern financial landscape. In this case study, we will explore recent contrarian triumphs—instances where savvy investors defied the prevailing sentiment, embraced contrarian principles, and reaped substantial rewards. These contemporary stories of success serve as powerful reminders that the contrarian approach is not only enduring but also highly relevant in today's dynamic markets.

## Contrarian Moves During Financial Crises

One of the defining characteristics of contrarian investors is their ability to remain calm amid financial storms and see opportunities when others see only chaos. The 2008 global financial crisis (GFC) provides an illuminating example of contrarian moves during times of extreme market turbulence.

As the GFC unfolded, panic and fear gripped the financial world. Most investors were rushing to the exits, selling their assets at distressed prices. However, contrarian investors took a different path. They recognized that the indiscriminate selling was creating opportunities in quality assets that had been unfairly battered.

### Key Point 1: The Contrarian Mindset During a Crisis

Contrarian investors during the GFC shared a common mindset. They understood that market corrections, even severe ones, are part of the natural ebb and flow of the financial markets. Instead of capitulating to fear, they saw the crisis as a chance to acquire assets that had the potential for significant future gains.

## Key Point 2: Identifying Value in the Midst of Panic

Contrarian investors during the crisis focused on asset valuation. They conducted thorough fundamental analyses to determine which companies had strong balance sheets, sustainable cash flows, and resilient business models. These contrarians sought out stocks trading at steep discounts to their intrinsic values.

## Key Point 3: Patiently Riding the Waves of Uncertainty

One hallmark of contrarian investors is their patience. They understood that the recovery from a financial crisis would not be immediate. Contrarians who weathered the storm by holding their well-researched positions were ultimately rewarded as markets rebounded.

Perhaps no investor epitomizes contrarian success during the financial crisis more than Warren Buffett. While many were panicking, Buffett was accumulating shares of major financial institutions, including Bank of America and Goldman Sachs, at deeply discounted prices. His contrarian move not only preserved his capital but also generated substantial returns when the banking sector recovered.

## The Rise of the 'FAANG' Contrarians

In recent years, a new breed of contrarians has emerged, challenging the prevailing wisdom regarding the so-called 'FAANG' stocks—Facebook, Apple, Amazon, Netflix, and Google (Alphabet). These technology giants have long been the darlings of Wall Street, with valuations that seemed to defy gravity. Yet, contrarian investors saw potential pitfalls in these soaring stocks.

### Key Point 1: Contrarian Skepticism in the Face of Exuberance

Contrarians observed that the valuations of FAANG stocks had reached astronomical levels, raising concerns about sustainability. They recognized that investor enthusiasm had driven prices to excessive levels, creating the potential for significant downside risk.

### Key Point 2: Timing Contrarian Moves Strategically

Contrarian investors in the FAANG stocks were not hasty in their decisions. They patiently awaited signs of vulnerability in these tech giants. When concerns about regulatory scrutiny, antitrust issues, or growth sustainability emerged, contrarians saw their entry points.

### Key Point 3: Navigating Contrarian Challenges

Investing against popular sentiment, especially when it comes to high-flying stocks, is not without its challenges.

Contrarians faced criticism and skepticism from those who believed the tech giants were unstoppable. However, their research, diligence, and conviction ultimately paid off.

**Figure 4 (Apple stock shows decline before making rebound in start of 2023)**

Apple, once the world's most valuable company, faced skepticism from contrarian investors who believed its growth story had peaked. Despite the prevailing narrative that Apple's best days were behind it, contrarians who recognized the company's cash reserves, loyal customer base, and ability to innovate made strategic investments. Apple's subsequent rise in market value vindicated their contrarian faith.

## Analyzing Recent Market Trends
Contrarian investors also adapt their strategies to changing market dynamics and trends. Recent years have witnessed

the rise of new asset classes, market phenomena, and global events that have shaped contrarian opportunities.

## Key Point 1: Cryptocurrencies and Contrarian Perspectives

The emergence of cryptocurrencies, led by Bitcoin, has presented contrarian investors with a unique set of challenges and opportunities. While some have embraced the digital revolution, contrarians have scrutinized the speculative fervor, regulatory uncertainties, and potential for bubbles. Some contrarians see value in blockchain technology while remaining cautious about the speculative aspects of crypto investing.

## Key Point 2: Contrarian Responses to Global Economic Shifts

Contrarian investors closely monitor global economic trends, geopolitical events, and macroeconomic shifts. Recent examples include contrarian moves driven by the U.S.-China trade tensions, Brexit, and the COVID-19 pandemic. These events created contrarian opportunities in sectors affected by market volatility and uncertainty.

## Key Point 3: Environmental, Social, and Governance (ESG) Contrarian Strategies

As ESG investing gains prominence, contrarian investors have explored contrarian approaches within this framework. They look for companies with strong ESG practices that may be overlooked by investors solely focused on ESG metrics. Contrarians in the ESG space also assess the potential for market overvaluation in popular ESG-themed assets.

In this dynamic investing landscape, contrarians adapt their strategies to seize opportunities, regardless of whether they challenge prevailing trends or align with emerging ones. The ability to recognize value, exercise patience, and maintain conviction in the face of skepticism remains at the heart of contrarian triumphs in the modern era. These case studies serve as living proof that contrarian investing is not bound by time; it's a timeless approach that continues to thrive in the ever-evolving world of finance.

# Chapter 7: Advanced Contrarian Strategies

## 7.1 Contrarian Signals in Market Trends

In the realm of contrarian investing, success hinges on the ability to perceive subtle, often overlooked signals amid the cacophony of market noise. This subchapter is your guide to identifying these contrarian signals, using technical indicators to refine your timing, and employing sector rotation strategies to seize contrarian opportunities.

### Identifying Contrarian Signals in Bull and Bear Markets

Contrarian investing thrives on spotting reversals or shifts in market sentiment before the majority catch on. This is where contrarian signals play a pivotal role.

### Contrarian Signals in Bull Markets:

1. Overbought Conditions: Bull markets often lead to excessively optimistic sentiment and overbought conditions. Contrarians watch for signs of extreme bullishness, such as high levels of speculation or soaring valuations, as potential contrarian sell signals.

2. Analyst Consensus: When financial analysts are overwhelmingly bullish on an asset or sector, it can be a warning sign for contrarians. Contrarian investors take note when consensus becomes too one-sided, as it suggests that the positive news is likely priced in.

3. Irrational Exuberance: Legendary investor Warren Buffett coined the term "irrational exuberance" to describe

periods of extreme optimism. Contrarians seek moments when euphoria reigns supreme, often signifying the peak of a bull market.

**Contrarian Signals in Bear Markets:**

1. Oversold Conditions: In bear markets, panic can lead to oversold conditions where assets are undervalued. Contrarians look for signs of extreme pessimism and selling exhaustion as potential contrarian buy signals.

2. Negative Headlines: When negative news dominates the headlines, it can create a sense of despair. Contrarians consider this pervasive negativity as a potential sign of a market bottom, as it suggests that bad news may already be priced in.

3. Capitulation: Capitulation occurs when investors give up hope and sell their positions en masse. Contrarians watch for signs of capitulation, as it can indicate that selling pressure is reaching its climax.

## Using Technical Indicators for Timing Contrarian Moves

Technical analysis is a valuable tool in the contrarian investor's arsenal, helping refine entry and exit points. Here are key technical indicators contrarians employ:

1. Relative Strength Index (RSI): The RSI measures the speed and change of price movements. Contrarians watch

for assets with RSI values below 30, indicating potential oversold conditions, or above 70, signaling potential overbought conditions.

**Figure 5 (Moving Average 25 and 260 Cross on Alphabet)**

2. Moving Averages: Moving averages smooth out price data over a specified period. Contrarians use moving averages to identify trends and potential trend reversals. For example, a "death cross" occurs when the short-term moving average crosses below the long-term moving average, signaling a potential downtrend.

3. Bollinger Bands: Bollinger Bands consist of a middle band (usually a 20-day moving average) and two standard deviation bands. Contrarians look for price moves that breach the bands, as they can signal overextended conditions.

4. Volume Analysis: Contrarians consider trading volume alongside price movements. Unusual spikes in volume,

especially during price reversals, can indicate strong contrarian signals.

5. Contrarian Oscillators: Some technical indicators are specifically designed for contrarian analysis. The "Smart Money Flow Index," for instance, tracks price and volume to distinguish between retail and institutional investors' actions, offering potential contrarian insights.

**Contrarian Sector Rotation Strategies**
In addition to timing individual asset moves, contrarian investors employ sector rotation strategies to capitalize on broader market trends. This approach involves shifting investments among different sectors based on their relative strength or weakness. Here's how contrarian sector rotation strategies work:

1. Spotting Sector Disparities: Contrarians assess sectors to identify those that are overvalued and poised for a downturn (contrarian sell) or undervalued and ripe for a rebound (contrarian buy).

2. Economic Cycle Analysis: Contrarians analyze economic cycles to anticipate which sectors might perform well in different phases. For example, during an economic recovery, they may favor cyclical sectors like industrials and technology.

3. Contrarian Sentiment: Contrarian investors gauge sector sentiment to identify sectors where pessimism has reached extremes. When everyone else is fleeing a sector, contrarians may see it as an opportunity.

4. Diversification: Contrarian sector rotation is a form of diversification. By spreading investments across sectors, contrarians reduce risk and improve their chances of capturing outperforming sectors.

5. Regular Reassessment: Contrarian sector rotation is not a static strategy. Investors regularly reassess sector strength and make adjustments to their portfolio allocations based on changing conditions.

The ability to identify contrarian signals, employ technical indicators, and execute sector rotation strategies is a hallmark of a seasoned contrarian investor. While contrarian investing demands patience and discipline, mastering these tools can help you navigate the ebb and flow of markets with precision. As you embark on your contrarian journey, remember that successful contrarian investing isn't about blindly defying the crowd; it's about recognizing when the crowd's sentiment has strayed from reality and seizing the contrarian opportunities that lie beneath the surface.

## 7.2 Risk Management in Contrarian Investing

In the high-stakes world of contrarian investing, where the pursuit of value often leads to diverging paths from the market consensus, the art of risk management takes center stage. Contrarian investors are not gamblers; they are calculated risk-takers who understand that protecting capital is just as important as seeking out undervalued opportunities. In this subchapter, we delve deep into the intricacies of risk management in contrarian investing, exploring strategies such as contrarian stop-loss and take-profit techniques, position sizing principles, and the judicious use of margin and leverage.

**Contrarian Stop-Loss and Take-Profit Strategies**

Contrarian investing is not a reckless endeavor where investors simply buy when others sell and vice versa. Contrarians meticulously manage their positions, and a key tool in their arsenal is the stop-loss order.

Stop-Loss Orders: Contrarian investors use stop-loss orders to limit potential losses. A stop-loss is a predetermined price at which an asset is automatically sold to prevent further losses. The logic behind this strategy is simple: contrarians recognize that not every contrarian move will be a winner, and it's essential to protect capital when an investment goes against them.

However, contrarian stop-losses are not set arbitrarily. They are often placed strategically, taking into account the asset's volatility and the investor's risk tolerance. Contrarians may set their stop-loss below a key support level or a technical indicator, such as a moving average, to minimize the chances of being whipsawed out of a position by short-term market fluctuations.

Take-Profit Strategies: On the flip side, contrarians also employ take-profit strategies to secure gains when an investment performs exceptionally well. These are predefined price levels at which an investor decides to exit a position to lock in profits. Contrarians understand the psychology of the market, and they know that even contrarian investments can become overvalued.

In practice, take-profit levels are set based on factors such as technical resistance levels, fundamental value targets, or the achievement of specific investment goals. By adhering to these predefined exit points, contrarians avoid the temptation to get greedy and hold onto an investment for too long, potentially giving back hard-earned gains.


## Position Sizing for Contrarian Portfolios

Another critical aspect of risk management in contrarian investing is position sizing. Position sizing refers to determining how much capital to allocate to a specific investment. Contrarians are keenly aware that diversification alone does not mitigate risk; it's the size of each position that truly matters.

The Power of Diversification: Contrarian investors often maintain diversified portfolios to spread risk. Diversification involves holding a mix of assets across different industries, sectors, and even asset classes. This diversification minimizes the impact of poor performance in one area, as losses in one position can be offset by gains in others.

Balancing Risk and Reward: Contrarians carefully balance the risk and reward of each position. A key principle in position sizing is to ensure that the potential reward justifies the risk taken. Positions in assets perceived as higher risk may receive smaller allocations, while those with a more favorable risk-reward profile can receive larger allocations.

Managing Concentration Risk: While diversification is essential, contrarians also understand the dangers of over-diversification. Holding too many positions can dilute the potential impact of winning investments. Therefore, they strike a balance between diversification and concentration to maximize the benefits of both.

## Managing Margin and Leverage with a Contrarian Approach

Margin trading and leverage can amplify both gains and losses, making them powerful tools in contrarian investing if used judiciously. However, they can also expose investors to significant risks, making it crucial for contrarians to employ these tools cautiously.

Margin Trading: Contrarians may use margin accounts to borrow funds to invest in additional assets. This leverage can amplify profits when contrarian moves are successful, but it also increases losses if investments move against them. Contrarians set strict rules for margin trading, including predefined margin call levels to prevent excessive losses.

Leveraged ETFs and Options: Some contrarians utilize leveraged exchange-traded funds (ETFs) or options to magnify their contrarian positions. These instruments provide enhanced exposure to the underlying asset's price movements. However, they come with their own set of complexities and risks, including decay in leveraged ETFs and the limited lifespan of options contracts.

Risk of Margin Calls: A contrarian's worst nightmare is a margin call, where the broker demands additional funds to cover potential losses. Contrarians avoid this scenario by maintaining ample cash reserves to meet margin requirements and by setting conservative margin levels to ensure positions remain solvent.

In the world of contrarian investing, risk management is not an afterthought but a core pillar of success. Contrarian stop-loss and take-profit strategies protect capital, position sizing principles ensure prudent allocation of resources, and the cautious use of margin and leverage amplifies gains while mitigating potential pitfalls. It's through this careful orchestration of risk management techniques that contrarian investors navigate the treacherous waters of market divergence, emerging not only unscathed but often with significant profits to show for their contrarian convictions.

## 7.3 Unconventional Contrarian Strategies

In the realm of contrarian investing, thinking outside the box is not merely encouraged; it's practically a prerequisite. While conventional wisdom often points to stocks and bonds as the primary avenues of investment, contrarian investors are known for their willingness to explore unconventional strategies and asset classes that diverge from the mainstream. In this subchapter, we embark on a journey into the fascinating world of unconventional contrarian strategies, where the daring and the discerning find opportunities that others overlook.

## Contrarian Investing in Alternative Assets

One hallmark of contrarian investors is their capacity to think beyond the traditional asset classes. They recognize that opportunities lie hidden in unconventional corners of the market, and they are more than willing to explore these unconventional options. Here are some alternative assets that contrarians often consider:

1. Real Assets: The realm of real assets includes tangible investments such as real estate, precious metals, and commodities. Contrarian investors see these assets as havens of value, particularly during times of market turbulence. Real estate, for instance, offers opportunities for contrarians to identify undervalued properties or markets poised for resurgence. Precious metals like gold and silver, historically seen as stores of value, can attract contrarians seeking to hedge against inflation or economic instability. Commodities, too, present contrarians with chances to capitalize on swings in supply and demand.

2. Cryptocurrencies: The emergence of cryptocurrencies represents a paradigm shift in the financial world. While it may seem unorthodox to some, contrarian investors

recognize the transformative potential of blockchain technology. They see cryptocurrencies as an unconventional but legitimate asset class. In their contrarian mindset, they identify opportunities in cryptocurrencies that have fallen out of favor but retain underlying utility and long-term potential. This might entail investing in projects with strong fundamentals or exploring emerging tokens and technologies.

3. Private Equity and Venture Capital: Contrarians are not confined to public markets; they are equally at home navigating the private investment landscape. They seek out opportunities in private equity or venture capital, often focusing on startups or companies that have been overlooked or underestimated by mainstream investors. This form of contrarian investment involves a longer-term horizon and higher risk tolerance but can yield substantial rewards for those who spot hidden gems.

4. Collectibles and Art: While some may view collectibles such as art, rare coins, or vintage cars as purely aesthetic pleasures, contrarians often view them as unconventional investment opportunities. These tangible assets may not generate regular income, but they have the potential to appreciate significantly over time. Contrarians with an eye for value and expertise in specific niches find success in this unconventional asset class. In the hands of the discerning contrarian, collectibles can be both aesthetically pleasing and financially rewarding.

## Contrarian Options and Derivatives Strategies

Options and derivatives may appear complex and esoteric to the average investor, but contrarians are undeterred by complexity. They understand that these financial instruments can be powerful tools when employed judiciously. Here's how contrarians harness options and derivatives:

1. Contrarian Covered Calls: Contrarian investors who hold stocks they believe are undervalued often engage in covered call writing. By selling covered call options on stocks they own, contrarians generate income in the form of premiums. Should the stock's price rise, they can still profit while waiting for the asset's value to appreciate further. This strategy enables contrarians to earn income while remaining invested in assets they expect to appreciate over time.

2. Contrarian Put Options: When contrarians perceive a stock as overvalued or foresee a potential correction, they may purchase put options as a form of insurance. Put options provide the holder with the right to sell a stock at a predetermined price within a specified time frame. In this way, contrarians safeguard against potential losses should the stock's price decline. Put options act as a financial safety net for contrarians, offering protection in bearish market scenarios.

3. Contrarian Straddle and Strangle Strategies: Contrarians employ straddle and strangle strategies when they anticipate significant price volatility but are uncertain about the direction of the price movement. These strategies

involve the simultaneous purchase of both call and put options with the same expiration date but different strike prices. In the case of a straddle, contrarians profit from a significant price movement in either direction, while in a strangle, they profit from an even more substantial price movement. These strategies can be highly effective when markets exhibit heightened uncertainty.

4. Contrarian Futures and Commodity Options: Contrarian investors with a deep understanding of commodity markets often use futures and options contracts to capitalize on price fluctuations. They look for opportunities in commodities that have fallen out of favor but exhibit potential for a rebound. By leveraging futures and options, contrarians gain exposure to commodities without owning the physical assets, thereby diversifying their portfolios and hedging against inflation or supply shocks.

## Contrarian Techniques for Short Selling and Hedging

The audacious practice of short selling—an approach that involves betting against the success of a security—is another tool in the contrarian arsenal. Here's a closer look at how contrarians utilize short selling:

1. Identifying Overvalued Assets: Contrarian short sellers are meticulous in their research and analysis. They scrutinize assets they believe to be overvalued, searching for signs of excessive speculation, unrealistic expectations, or unsustainable valuations. They possess a keen sense of

discernment, recognizing when market sentiment has inflated prices beyond reasonable levels.

2. Timing the Short Position: Timing is crucial for contrarian short sellers. They exercise patience, often waiting for clear indications that market sentiment is shifting or that an asset's fundamentals are deteriorating. Contrarians understand that short selling can be fraught with risk, as losses can be potentially unlimited if the asset's price rises. As such, they are exceptionally cautious and selective in their short-selling endeavors.

3. Hedging with Short Positions: Contrarians often employ short positions as a form of portfolio hedging. By maintaining short positions in assets that are expected to decline when their long positions are suffering losses, contrarians can mitigate the impact of market downturns. This hedging strategy is akin to a financial safety net, helping contrarians preserve capital and weather market turbulence.

4. Risk Management: Short selling entails inherent risks, and contrarian investors are well aware of these risks. To safeguard their portfolios, they implement rigorous risk management measures. This includes setting stop-loss orders to limit potential losses, monitoring their short positions vigilantly, and adjusting their strategies as market conditions evolve. Discipline is paramount, as short selling requires a steadfast commitment to risk management.

Contrarian investing is a multifaceted discipline, and its practitioners are not constrained by convention. By exploring unconventional assets, harnessing the power of options and derivatives, and engaging in short selling and hedging, contrarians expand their repertoire of strategies to navigate complex and dynamic markets. These advanced techniques are not for the faint of heart, but for those willing to delve into the uncharted waters of unconventional contrarian strategies, the potential rewards can be substantial. In the world of contrarian investing, innovation and adaptability are the hallmarks of success.

# Chapter 8: Exploring Specialized Contrarian Approaches

## 8.1 Behavioral Finance and Contrarian Strategies

In the realm of contrarian investing, the battle is not merely against market forces and economic fundamentals; it's also a psychological duel. The human psyche, fraught with behavioral biases and irrationality, often guides investor decisions in ways that seem contrary to logical, rational choices. In this subchapter, we dive deep into the fascinating intersection of behavioral finance and contrarian investing—a space where understanding human behavior becomes a formidable tool for reaping profits.

### Understanding Behavioral Biases in Contrarian Investing

Contrarian investing hinges on recognizing and exploiting behavioral biases that lead to market mispricing. Let's explore some of the most prevalent biases and how they intersect with contrarian strategies:

1. Herd Mentality: One of the most influential biases in markets is the tendency to follow the crowd. Contrarian investors are acutely aware of this bias and often act in direct opposition to it. When the majority of investors are buying feverishly, contrarians may be selling, and vice versa. They recognize that herding behavior can create market bubbles and crashes, which present contrarian opportunities.

2. Overconfidence: Investors frequently overestimate their knowledge and abilities. Contrarians remain humble in the face of uncertainty, acknowledging that markets are complex and unpredictable. They avoid the overconfidence trap and approach investing with a healthy dose of skepticism.

3. Confirmation Bias: Investors tend to seek information that confirms their existing beliefs and ignore contradictory evidence. Contrarians actively seek out dissenting opinions and data, challenging their assumptions and preventing confirmation bias from clouding their judgment.

4. Loss Aversion: The pain of losses is felt more profoundly than the joy of gains. Contrarians understand that fear of loss can lead to irrational selling during market downturns, creating buying opportunities. They are willing to endure short-term losses for the prospect of long-term gains.

5. Anchoring: Investors often anchor their decisions to specific price levels or past performance. Contrarians avoid being anchored to past prices and instead focus on current fundamentals and market sentiment.

**Contrarian Tactics Based on Investor Sentiment**
Contrarian investors keenly observe investor sentiment as a source of contrarian signals. Market sentiment is often a pendulum swinging between extremes of optimism and pessimism, providing ample contrarian opportunities:

1. Extreme Pessimism: When the market sentiment turns overwhelmingly negative, contrarians see a potential contrarian buy signal. Excessive fear can lead to indiscriminate selling, pushing prices below intrinsic values. Contrarians search for assets that have been unjustifiably beaten down and poised for a rebound.

2. Excessive Optimism: Conversely, when the market sentiment reaches euphoric levels, contrarians view this as a potential contrarian sell signal. Excessive optimism can drive asset prices to unsustainable heights, setting the stage for corrections. Contrarians may take profits or reduce exposure when others are overly bullish.

3. Sentiment Indicators: Contrarians utilize sentiment indicators, such as the VIX (Volatility Index) or surveys of investor sentiment, to gauge market sentiment. When these indicators reach extreme levels, they serve as valuable contrarian signals.

### How to Profit from Market Overreactions

Market overreactions are a fertile ground for contrarian investors seeking to capitalize on irrational behavior:

1. Overreaction to Bad News: When negative news triggers panic selling, contrarians evaluate whether the market's reaction is justified. If the fundamentals of an asset remain strong despite short-term challenges, contrarians may consider it a buying opportunity.

2. Overreaction to Good News: Conversely, markets can overreact positively to news, causing asset prices to

become overvalued. Contrarians exercise caution during such periods, assessing whether the positive sentiment is sustainable or likely to lead to a correction.

3. Contrarian Averaging: Contrarians may employ a strategy of dollar-cost averaging during market overreactions. This involves steadily buying assets at predetermined intervals, regardless of market sentiment. It allows contrarians to accumulate positions at favorable prices over time.

4. Value Investing: The value investing philosophy closely aligns with contrarian principles. Value investors seek undervalued assets, often those that have experienced market overreactions. Contrarian investors, too, focus on buying assets trading below their intrinsic value.

5. Long-Term Perspective: Contrarians adopt a long-term perspective, understanding that market overreactions tend to correct themselves over time. They have the patience to weather short-term volatility and capitalize on eventual price adjustments.

In the world of contrarian investing, behavioral finance is not just a theoretical concept; it's a practical tool that allows investors to navigate the treacherous waters of human psychology. By understanding the behavioral biases that influence market participants and by leveraging sentiment indicators, contrarians position themselves to profit from market overreactions and capitalize on the irrationality of others. Contrarian investing is not merely about going against the crowd; it's about exploiting the crowd's irrationality for your financial gain.

## 8.2 Seasonal Contrarian Investing

In the world of contrarian investing, there is a treasure trove of unconventional approaches waiting to be explored. One such strategy that stands out for its unique dynamics and profitable potential is Seasonal Contrarian Investing. This subchapter will be your guide to understanding, harnessing, and profiting from the fascinating world of seasonal market patterns.

### Leveraging Seasonal Patterns in Markets

Seasonal contrarian investing hinges on a simple yet powerful idea: markets have distinct patterns and behaviors that recur predictably during specific times of the year. These patterns are often rooted in human psychology, historical trends, and economic cycles. By recognizing and exploiting these seasonal tendencies, contrarian investors can position themselves to benefit from market movements that defy conventional wisdom.

Summer Lulls and Autumn Harvests: One common seasonal pattern in many markets is the summer lull followed by the autumn harvest. During the summer months, market activity tends to slow down as traders take vacations, leading to reduced trading volumes and sometimes lower volatility. Contrarians may use this period to analyze their portfolios, review their strategies, and prepare for potential opportunities in the fall.

Year-End Window Dressing: Toward the end of the calendar year, many institutional investors engage in a practice known as "window dressing." This involves selling underperforming assets and purchasing outperforming ones to improve the appearance of their year-end portfolio reports. Contrarian investors can benefit by identifying assets that have been unfairly sold off as part of this process.

Tax-Loss Harvesting: At the end of the year, some investors engage in tax-loss harvesting to offset capital gains with capital losses, reducing their tax liabilities. This can create temporary downward pressure on certain stocks, creating opportunities for contrarians to step in and buy undervalued assets.

## Strategies for Capitalizing on Year-End and Start-of-Year Effects

Now, let's delve into strategies that contrarian investors can employ to capitalize on these seasonal effects:

1. Tax-Loss Reaping: As the calendar year comes to a close, contrarian investors can sift through the wreckage of tax-loss harvesting. Identify stocks that have been unjustly beaten down due to this selling pressure but possess strong fundamentals. These can be prime candidates for contrarian buys.

2. Post-Holiday Rally: After the holiday season, particularly in January, markets often experience what's known as a "Santa Claus Rally" or "January Effect." This is a historical tendency for stocks to perform well in the early weeks of the year. Contrarians may strategically position themselves to benefit from this upward momentum.

3. Anticipating Market Cycles: Contrarian investors keen on market cycles may position themselves to anticipate seasonal fluctuations. For instance, they might adopt a more cautious stance as summer approaches and a more opportunistic one as the year-end draws near, aligning their portfolio with the ebb and flow of market sentiment.

## Contrarian Opportunities in Holiday-Driven Market Behavior

Holidays can bring not only joy and celebration but also unique contrarian investment opportunities. Let's explore a few holiday-driven market behaviors and how contrarians can harness them:

1. Holiday Shopping and Retail Stocks: The holiday season is synonymous with gift-giving and shopping sprees. Contrarians can evaluate retail stocks, especially those that may have faced temporary setbacks but are poised to benefit from increased consumer spending during the holidays.

2. Pre-Holiday Pessimism: In the run-up to certain holidays, markets can exhibit pre-holiday pessimism, as traders worry about potential disruptions. Contrarian

investors may see this as a chance to accumulate assets at lower prices, anticipating a post-holiday rebound.

3. The January Bounce: The start of a new year often ushers in optimism and resolutions, and this sentiment can extend to the markets. Contrarians who position themselves ahead of this January bounce may find themselves riding the wave of positive sentiment.

It's important to note that while seasonal contrarian investing can be lucrative, it is not without risks. Market behavior can deviate from historical patterns due to unforeseen events or changes in investor sentiment. Therefore, contrarian investors must combine their seasonal insights with robust fundamental and technical analysis to make informed decisions.

Seasonal contrarian investing offers a unique window of opportunity for those willing to venture beyond conventional strategies. By understanding and leveraging seasonal market patterns, contrarian investors can uncover hidden gems in unexpected places and turn the tides of market sentiment to their advantage. As you delve deeper into the world of contrarian investing, consider adding the dynamic strategy of seasonal analysis to your arsenal, and watch how the seasons can become a source of profitable wisdom in your investment journey.

## 8.3 The Art of Contrarian Value Investing

Contrarian investing isn't a monolithic strategy; it's a multifaceted approach with various nuances, each designed to uncover hidden gems in the market. Among these nuanced strategies, Contrarian Value Investing stands tall as a time-tested method for identifying undervalued assets and building long-term wealth. In this subchapter, we'll dissect the art of Contrarian Value Investing, exploring how to identify undervalued assets using contrarian principles, the essential contrarian value metrics and ratios, and how to construct a robust, long-term wealth strategy rooted in value contrarianism.

### Identifying Undervalued Assets with Contrarian Principles

At the heart of Contrarian Value Investing is the belief that market sentiment often overshoots, pushing asset prices to extremes—both undervalued and overvalued. Contrarian Value Investors focus on the former, searching for assets that have been unjustly neglected or beaten down by market forces. Here's how they go about identifying such opportunities:

1. Screening for Neglected Sectors: Contrarian Value Investors cast their nets in sectors or industries that have fallen out of favor. This often involves sectors facing temporary headwinds or negative sentiment, where valuable companies may be trading at bargain prices.

2. Analyzing Fundamentals: Contrarians dive deep into the fundamentals of potential investments. They scrutinize

financial statements, earnings reports, and cash flows to determine the intrinsic value of a company. Contrarian investors seek companies with strong financials that are temporarily undervalued.

3. Contrarian Sentiment Analysis: While Contrarian Value Investors are focused on fundamentals, they are not oblivious to sentiment. They look for signs that pessimism has reached extreme levels, signaling a potential contrarian buying opportunity.

4. Scouring for Contrarian Catalysts: Contrarian investors are on the lookout for catalysts that can change market sentiment. This could be a new product launch, a change in management, or an industry-wide shift that could turn the tide in favor of the undervalued asset.


**Contrarian Value Metrics and Ratios**
To identify undervalued assets, Contrarian Value Investors rely on a set of key metrics and ratios that provide insights into a company's financial health and valuation. Here are some of the most crucial ones:

1. Price-to-Earnings (P/E) Ratio: The P/E ratio compares a company's stock price to its earnings per share. A low P/E ratio relative to the industry or historical averages can indicate an undervalued stock.

2. Price-to-Book (P/B) Ratio: The P/B ratio compares a company's stock price to its book value (total assets minus total liabilities). A P/B ratio below 1 suggests the stock may be undervalued.

3. Price-to-Sales (P/S) Ratio: The P/S ratio compares a company's stock price to its revenue per share. A low P/S ratio may indicate an undervalued stock.

4. Dividend Yield: Contrarian Value Investors often seek stocks with attractive dividend yields. A high dividend yield can indicate that the stock is undervalued, and the company is returning value to shareholders.

5. Earnings Yield: The earnings yield is the reciprocal of the P/E ratio and represents the return on investment from earnings. A higher earnings yield suggests better value.

6. Free Cash Flow: Examining a company's free cash flow, which is the cash left after operating expenses and capital expenditures, helps Contrarian Value Investors assess a company's financial stability and growth potential.

**Building a Long-Term Wealth Strategy with Value Contrarianism**

Contrarian Value Investing is not a get-rich-quick scheme; it's a patient and disciplined approach to wealth accumulation. Here's how Contrarian Value Investors construct a long-term wealth-building strategy:

1. Diversification: Contrarian Value Investors spread their investments across different sectors and industries to reduce risk. Diversification ensures that a poor-performing investment in one sector doesn't significantly impact the overall portfolio.

2. Buy and Hold: Contrarian Value Investors are typically long-term investors. They buy undervalued assets with the intention of holding them for an extended period, allowing time for the market to recognize their value.

3. Reinvestment: As value is realized in their investments, Contrarian Value Investors often reinvest the proceeds into new undervalued assets. This strategy compounds wealth over time.

4. Staying Informed: Contrarian Value Investors stay well-informed about their investments and the broader market. They continuously monitor their portfolio and adjust their positions as needed based on changing circumstances.

5. Risk Management: While Contrarian Value Investors seek undervalued assets, they are not blind to risk. They assess the risk-reward ratio of each investment and employ risk management techniques, such as stop-loss orders, to protect their capital.

6. Patience and Discipline: One of the key virtues of Contrarian Value Investing is patience. Contrarian Value Investors are prepared to weather short-term volatility and hold their investments until the underlying value is recognized.

7. Income Generation: Some Contrarian Value Investors focus on income generation by investing in dividend-paying stocks. The income generated can provide financial stability and reinvestment opportunities.

Contrarian Value Investing is a powerful strategy for identifying undervalued assets and building long-term wealth. It combines a deep analysis of fundamentals, contrarian sentiment analysis, and a disciplined, patient approach to investing. By mastering the art of Contrarian Value Investing, you can potentially unlock substantial profits while mitigating risk in your investment journey.

# Chapter 9: Integrating Options with Your Contrarian Portfolio

## 9.1 Options and Asset Allocation in Contrarian Investing

Options, often viewed as intricate financial instruments, are an essential tool in the contrarian investor's toolkit. They provide the flexibility to tailor strategies to specific market conditions, offering opportunities for profit and risk management. In this subchapter, we'll explore how contrarian investors can seamlessly integrate options into their portfolios, enhancing diversification, managing risk, and optimizing their investment approach.

### Diversification Strategies with Contrarian Options

Diversification is a fundamental principle of prudent investing. It involves spreading your investments across different asset classes to reduce risk and enhance the potential for returns. Contrarian investors, while known for their selective approach, also recognize the value of diversification, and options can play a pivotal role in this regard.

1. Covered Calls: One popular contrarian options strategy is covered calls. Here, an investor holds a long position in an underlying asset (typically a stock) and simultaneously sells call options on that asset. The call options provide income through premiums, while the underlying asset remains in the portfolio. It's a way to generate additional

income from existing holdings while maintaining exposure to potential capital gains.

2. Protective Puts: Contrarian investors can also use protective puts to hedge their positions. A protective put involves purchasing put options on an existing holding. If the asset's price declines significantly, the put options act as insurance, allowing the investor to sell the asset at a predetermined strike price, mitigating potential losses.

3. Straddle and Strangle Strategies: These strategies involve buying both call and put options on the same asset with the same expiration date. Contrarian investors may use these strategies when they expect significant price volatility but are uncertain about the direction. Straddles involve at-the-money options, while strangles use out-of-the-money options. These strategies can provide opportunities for profit in volatile market conditions.

4. Options on Contrarian Assets: Contrarian investors can use options directly on assets that are out of favor or undervalued. For instance, they might purchase call options on a stock they believe is poised for a contrarian rally or sell put options on assets they are willing to acquire at a lower price. These strategies allow contrarians to leverage their convictions while managing risk.

**Balancing Risk and Reward in Your Portfolio**
Effective contrarian investing with options is about achieving a delicate balance between risk and reward. While options can enhance returns and provide downside

protection, they also introduce their own set of risks. Here's how contrarian investors balance these factors:

1. Risk Assessment: Before incorporating options, contrarian investors thoroughly assess their risk tolerance and overall portfolio risk. They consider how options may impact their risk profile and whether the potential benefits align with their investment goals.

2. Position Sizing: Contrarians carefully manage the size of their options positions relative to their overall portfolio. They avoid overextending themselves, ensuring that options do not dominate the portfolio's risk profile.

3. Strategic Timing: Timing is critical when executing options strategies. Contrarians are patient and choose strategic entry and exit points for their options positions. They align options strategies with their contrarian convictions, maximizing their potential impact.

4. Continuous Monitoring: Contrarian investors actively monitor their options positions and adjust them as market conditions evolve. This proactive approach allows them to respond to changing circumstances and market dynamics effectively.

### Developing an Options-Centric Portfolio Approach
Contrarian investors often evolve toward an options-centric portfolio approach as they gain experience and confidence in options trading. This approach leverages the unique characteristics of options to enhance contrarian strategies:

1. Income Generation: Options can generate income through premiums. Contrarian investors may use covered calls, cash-secured puts, or other income-generating strategies to supplement their portfolio's returns.

2. Risk Management: Options provide an array of risk management tools. Contrarians may use protective puts, collars, or other strategies to limit potential losses in their portfolio.

3. Leverage: While contrarian investing is typically conservative, options allow for controlled leverage. Contrarians can amplify their positions in undervalued assets with limited risk through options.

4. Flexibility: Options offer flexibility in adapting to changing market conditions. Contrarians can adjust their options positions to capitalize on contrarian opportunities or protect against potential downturns.

5. Income during Market Downturns: Contrarian investors who hold a contrarian view during bear markets can use options to generate income while they wait for market sentiment to align with their contrarian perspective.

6. Portfolio Tailoring: Contrarian investors can tailor options strategies to specific assets or market conditions, allowing for a customized approach to contrarian investing.

Options can be a valuable addition to the contrarian investor's toolkit, providing diversification, risk management, and potential enhancements to returns.

However, options trading requires a deep understanding of the instrument and a commitment to disciplined risk management. When used strategically and in alignment with contrarian principles, options can be a powerful ally in the pursuit of contrarian investing success.

## 9.2 Risk Management and Options in Contrarian Portfolios

In the world of contrarian investing, where the terrain can be as unpredictable as it is lucrative, managing risk is paramount. While contrarians are known for their willingness to swim against the current, they are also keenly aware that not every contrarian bet will turn into gold. In this subchapter, we delve into the art of using options to fine-tune risk management within your contrarian portfolio.

### Portfolio Protection with Contrarian Options

The ability to protect a contrarian portfolio from unexpected downturns is a valuable skill, and options offer a range of protective mechanisms:

1. Hedging Against Market Declines: Contrarian investors recognize that market downturns are part of the investment landscape. By purchasing put options on broad market indices, they can hedge their entire portfolio against systemic risk. If the market falls, the put options will

appreciate in value, offsetting potential losses in their holdings.

2. Sector-Specific Hedging: For contrarians who focus on specific sectors or industries, sector-specific index options can serve as a hedge. By holding put options on indices related to their sector of interest, they can protect their portfolio from sector-specific risks.

3. Diversified Portfolio Hedging: Contrarians with diversified portfolios can use a combination of put options on individual holdings to create a custom-tailored hedge. By strategically selecting which assets to protect, they can minimize risk while still capitalizing on the growth potential of other holdings.

4. Dynamic Hedging: Contrarian investors understand that market conditions can change rapidly. As such, they may employ a dynamic hedging strategy, adjusting their options positions as market conditions evolve. This flexibility allows them to respond to changing risks and opportunities in real-time.

Options provide contrarians with the ability to guard their portfolios against adverse market movements without necessarily liquidating their positions. This strategic approach ensures that they remain in the game, ready to seize contrarian opportunities as they arise.

**Strategies for Handling Market Volatility**
Contrarian investing often thrives amidst market volatility, but it's not without its challenges. Options can play a

pivotal role in helping contrarians navigate turbulent markets:

1. Volatility Trading: Contrarians recognize that increased market volatility can create opportunities. By trading options strategies that capitalize on volatility, such as straddles or strangles, they can profit from significant price swings.

2. Selling Premium: During periods of heightened volatility, option premiums tend to rise. Contrarians may take advantage of this by selling options and collecting premiums. For instance, selling covered calls on volatile stocks can generate income while mitigating downside risk.

3. Volatility Skew Awareness: Contrarians are attuned to the volatility skew, which refers to the varying implied volatilities of options with different strike prices. They use this knowledge to identify undervalued or overvalued options and construct positions that align with their contrarian views.

4. Earnings Season Strategies: Earnings season often introduces heightened volatility as companies report their financial results. Contrarians may employ options strategies, such as iron condors or straddles, to profit from the uncertainty and price fluctuations surrounding earnings announcements.

Market volatility, far from being a deterrent, is a fertile ground for contrarian investors. By strategically using options to manage and capitalize on volatility, they position themselves to thrive in even the most tumultuous market conditions.

Incorporating options into your contrarian portfolio is akin to adding a finely tuned instrument to an orchestra. It allows for precise control and adjustment of risk while preserving the harmony of your investment strategy. As we delve further into the world of contrarian investing, remember that options are not merely instruments of complexity but powerful tools of risk management, enabling you to execute your contrarian vision with greater precision and confidence.

## 9.3 Timing and Execution of Contrarian Options Trades

Options trading, when combined with a contrarian approach, can open a world of possibilities for savvy investors. It's a strategy that goes beyond conventional stock trading, offering a unique set of tools to capitalize on market inefficiencies. In this subchapter, we'll explore the critical aspects of timing and executing contrarian options trades, including finding the right moments to enter and exit positions, tactical considerations, and the unwavering discipline required for success.

## Timing Contrarian Options Buys and Sells

Timing is the linchpin of successful options trading within a contrarian framework. Contrarian options traders don't merely buy calls or puts arbitrarily; they analyze market conditions, asset trends, and sentiment indicators to identify opportune moments for options trades.

* Assessing Market Sentiment: Contrarian options traders pay close attention to market sentiment. They look for extremes in bullish or bearish sentiment as potential contrarian signals. For instance, when optimism reaches irrational levels, contrarians may consider buying put options as a contrarian bet against the prevailing sentiment.

* Monitoring Volatility: Options prices are heavily influenced by market volatility. Contrarians analyze volatility indicators, such as the VIX (CBOE Volatility Index), to gauge the level of fear or complacency in the market. High volatility may present opportunities for options trades, as prices are more likely to experience significant fluctuations.

* Evaluating Asset Trends: Contrarian options strategies often involve taking positions contrary to the prevailing trend. Traders analyze price charts and technical indicators to identify potential trend reversals. This is crucial for determining whether to buy call options in a bearish trend or put options in a bullish trend.

* Event Timing: Contrarian options traders keep an eye on economic events, earnings releases, and geopolitical developments. These events can trigger market shifts and create opportunities for contrarian options trades. For

instance, contrarians may use options to hedge against unexpected market reactions to earnings reports.

**Tactical Entry and Exit Points with Options**
Executing options trades effectively requires a tactical approach. Contrarian options traders use a variety of tactics to time their entries and exits, aiming to maximize profit potential while managing risk:

* Use of Technical Analysis: Contrarian options traders employ technical analysis to pinpoint entry and exit levels. They identify support and resistance levels, trendlines, and chart patterns that can serve as tactical entry and exit points.

* Setting Price Targets: Before entering an options trade, contrarians set price targets based on their analysis. These targets guide their exit strategy. For example, if they buy call options expecting a stock to rebound, they may set a price target at a level where they believe the contrarian move is exhausted.

* Implementing Stop-Loss Orders: Managing risk is paramount in options trading. Contrarian options traders use stop-loss orders to limit potential losses. These orders automatically sell options positions if they reach a predetermined price, helping to prevent significant losses.

* Rolling Options Positions: Options have finite lifetimes, and their values decay over time. Contrarian options traders may roll their positions by closing out expiring options and opening new ones with later expiration dates. This tactic

allows them to maintain exposure to contrarian moves while mitigating time decay.

* Scaling In and Out: Contrarian options traders may scale into positions by gradually building their options portfolio as their conviction grows. Similarly, they can scale out of positions by gradually reducing exposure as their price targets are met.

## Staying Disciplined in Options-Based Contrarian Strategies

Options trading can be alluring but also fraught with complexity and risk. Discipline is the foundation of success in options-based contrarian strategies:

* Adhering to a Trading Plan: Contrarian options traders follow a well-defined trading plan that includes entry and exit criteria, risk management rules, and position sizing guidelines. Deviating from the plan can lead to costly mistakes.

* Risk Management: Options trading carries inherent risks, including the potential loss of the entire premium paid. Contrarian options traders manage risk by carefully selecting position sizes, setting stop-loss orders, and diversifying their options portfolio.

* Continuous Learning: Options markets are dynamic, and new strategies and products emerge regularly. Contrarian options traders commit to ongoing education, staying informed about changes in the options landscape and evolving their strategies accordingly.

* Emotional Control: Options trading can be emotionally taxing, especially during periods of volatility. Contrarian options traders practice emotional control, avoiding impulsive decisions driven by fear or greed.

* Reviewing and Adjusting Strategies: Contrarian options traders periodically review their trading strategies to assess their effectiveness. They adjust their approaches based on performance metrics and lessons learned from previous trades.

Contrarian options trading is not for the faint of heart, but for those who master its intricacies, it offers a potent toolset for profiting in volatile or irrational markets. By carefully timing and executing options trades with discipline, contrarian investors can navigate market uncertainty with confidence and seize opportunities that others may overlook.

# Chapter 10: Leveraging Index Options in Contrarian Investing

## 10.1 Introduction to Index Options

In the realm of contrarian investing, where unconventional strategies often lead to extraordinary profits, one tool stands out as a hidden gem: index options. These financial instruments hold the potential to elevate your contrarian investing game, providing a unique avenue to exploit market inefficiencies and capitalize on sentiment-driven market movements. In this subchapter, we will embark on a journey to demystify index options, shedding light on their significance, types, and the pivotal role they play in the contrarian investor's toolkit.

### Understanding Index Options and Their Significance

Before delving into the intricacies of index options, let's establish a fundamental understanding of what they are and why they hold immense significance in the world of contrarian investing.

### *What Are Index Options?*

At its core, an index option is a financial derivative that derives its value from the performance of an underlying market index, such as the S&P 500, the Dow Jones Industrial Average, or the Nasdaq 100. Unlike individual stock options, which are based on the performance of a single company, index options provide exposure to the broader market, making them a valuable tool for contrarian investors seeking to navigate market sentiment and trends.

**\*The Significance of Index Options in Contrarian Investing\***

Index options serve as a unique lens through which contrarian investors can analyze market sentiment on a grand scale. These options allow you to bet on the overall direction of the market or specific market segments, rather than picking individual stocks. Here are some key reasons why index options are significant in contrarian investing:

1. Broad Market Exposure: Index options provide exposure to the performance of a diversified portfolio of stocks. This means you can capitalize on broader market trends without the need to analyze and select individual companies—a significant advantage for contrarians seeking to mitigate risks associated with single-stock investments.

2. Contrarian Signals: Market sentiment often swings from extreme optimism to pessimism. Index options reflect these shifts, and contrarian investors can use them to identify overbought or oversold conditions in the market as a whole. When the majority of investors are overly bullish or bearish, it can signal a contrarian opportunity.

3. Hedging and Risk Management: Index options offer a valuable tool for managing risk. Contrarian investors can use them to hedge their portfolios during times of uncertainty or to protect gains during market downturns. This risk management aspect aligns well with the

contrarian philosophy of preserving capital in adverse conditions.


### Types of Index Options: Calls and Puts

Now that we grasp the essence of index options, it's time to explore their two primary forms: calls and puts. Understanding these options is crucial for contrarian investors, as they offer distinct strategies and opportunities for profiting from market moves.


### *Index Call Options*

Index call options give the holder the right, but not the obligation, to buy the underlying index at a specified strike price before a predetermined expiration date. Contrarian investors often use index call options in the following ways:

- Betting on Market Upside: When contrarians anticipate a market upswing after a prolonged decline or during a correction phase, they can buy index call options. These options allow them to profit from the expected rise in the index's value without committing to purchasing the actual stocks.

- Capitalizing on Bullish Sentiment: Index call options become particularly attractive when contrarian investors detect a shift in market sentiment from pessimism to optimism. By purchasing call options, they participate in potential market rallies while preserving capital.

- Leveraging Market Reversals: During bear markets or severe corrections, contrarian investors may anticipate a sharp rebound. Index call options offer leverage, magnifying potential gains if the market indeed experiences a rapid recovery.

### *Index Put Options*

Conversely, index put options grant the holder the right, but not the obligation, to sell the underlying index at a specified strike price before a predetermined expiration date. Contrarian investors often employ index put options for the following purposes:

- Protecting Portfolios: When contrarians foresee market downturns or increased volatility, they can purchase index put options as a form of portfolio insurance. These options allow them to profit from declining market values, offsetting losses in their stock holdings.

- Capitalizing on Bearish Sentiment: Contrarian investors are not limited to betting on market rallies; they can also profit from bearish sentiment. When they anticipate a significant market decline, index put options provide a way to benefit from falling index values.

- Managing Risk: Index put options offer a strategic tool for contrarian investors to limit potential losses during market uncertainties. By purchasing puts, they can define their maximum risk exposure while retaining the flexibility to participate in potential gains.

**The Role of Index Options in Contrarian Investing**

As we navigate the landscape of contrarian investing, it becomes evident that index options serve as indispensable instruments for contrarian investors. They offer a means to capitalize on market sentiment, hedge against risks, and strategically position portfolios for contrarian opportunities.

**\*Contrarian Signals in Index Options\***

Index options often exhibit distinct patterns and pricing anomalies that contrarian investors keenly observe. For instance, when a significant portion of market participants piles into call options, anticipating a relentless rally, it can signal excessive optimism—a contrarian red flag. Conversely, a surge in put option buying may suggest widespread fear and a potential contrarian buy opportunity.

**\*Strategies for Contrarian Investors\***

Contrarian investors employ a variety of strategies using index options, depending on their market outlook and risk tolerance:

1. Bullish Contrarian Strategies: Contrarians may buy index call options when they foresee a market upswing, aiming to profit from rising index values. This strategy allows them to participate in potential rallies while minimizing capital commitment.

2. Bearish Contrarian Strategies: When contrarian investors anticipate market declines, they can purchase index put options as a hedge or to profit from falling index values. This approach enables them to navigate bearish sentiment effectively.

3. Volatility Contrarian Strategies: Contrarian investors can also focus on market volatility. They may use options strategies like straddles or strangles to profit from significant price swings, which often accompany contrarian opportunities.

4. Portfolio Protection: Index put options serve as an essential tool for protecting portfolios during adverse market conditions. Contrarian investors can use them to safeguard their gains and mitigate losses.

In essence, index options offer contrarian investors the ability to tactically position themselves in the market— whether it's to take advantage of changing sentiment, protect their portfolios, or profit from market gyrations. Contrarian investing is not merely about going against the crowd; it's about using every available tool to thrive in a world where opportunities often hide in plain sight.

## 10.2 Implementing Contrarian Strategies with Index Options

In the world of contrarian investing, mastering the art of timing is paramount. Contrarians understand that markets have their ebb and flow, and this rhythm often manifests through index movements. In this subchapter, we'll explore how index options can be leveraged to implement contrarian strategies effectively. We'll delve into recognizing contrarian signals within index movements, deciphering overbought and oversold conditions using index options, and the strategic use of index put options for both hedging and contrarian bearish plays.

### Contrarian Signals in Index Movements

To embark on a journey into the world of contrarian strategies with index options, one must first develop a keen eye for contrarian signals within index movements. Indices, such as the S&P 500 or the Dow Jones Industrial Average, encapsulate the collective sentiment of the market. As such, they often serve as early indicators of impending market shifts.

1. Overextended Bull Runs: Contrarian investors keep a watchful eye for signs of overextended bull markets where indices experience prolonged periods of unrelenting growth. Such exuberance can often lead to overvaluation, paving the way for a potential correction. Recognizing when an index has gone too far too fast can be a contrarian's cue to consider protective measures.

**Figure 6 (Decline of S&P 500 and opportunity to buy)**

2. Abrupt Index Declines: Conversely, contrarians are poised to act when indices experience sharp declines. While the market may panic, the contrarian remains vigilant, searching for signs of excessive pessimism and the potential for an oversold rebound. Abrupt index declines can signal a contrarian opportunity to initiate bullish positions.

3. Divergence Between Indices: Another valuable contrarian signal lies in the divergence between different indices. When one index outperforms while others languish, it can signal a disconnect between sectors or asset classes. Contrarians interpret this as a potential contrarian opportunity, considering rebalancing strategies to capitalize on market misalignments.

## Understanding Overbought and Oversold based on Index Options

Index options offer a unique window into assessing whether an index is overbought or oversold. These conditions can serve as contrarian signals for astute investors.

1. Overbought Conditions: When an index experiences an extended period of bullishness, option premiums on call options may surge. This increased demand for call options can drive up their prices, resulting in high implied volatility. Contrarians often interpret this as an indication that the index is overbought, and a correction may be looming.

2. Oversold Conditions: On the flip side, during bearish market phases, put options become more sought after. Increased demand for put options can inflate their premiums, leading to elevated implied volatility. Contrarians recognize this as a potential oversold condition, signaling that the index may be due for a rebound.

3. Volatility Skew: The options market can provide insights into market sentiment. A significant skew in implied volatility between call and put options can indicate the overall sentiment regarding the index. For instance, if put options exhibit notably higher implied volatility than call options, it may imply a bearish sentiment among investors.


## Using Index Put Options for Hedging and Contrarian Bearish Plays

One of the hallmark strategies employed by contrarians in their arsenal of index options is the strategic use of index put options. These options provide a means to hedge against potential market downturns and implement contrarian bearish plays.

1. Hedging with Index Put Options: Contrarian investors use index put options as a form of insurance. When they anticipate a potential market correction, they purchase index put options. If the market does indeed take a downturn, these put options appreciate in value, offsetting losses in the overall portfolio. This strategy allows contrarians to safeguard their investments while staying positioned for potential contrarian opportunities.

2. Bearish Plays: Contrarians also leverage index put options to capitalize on their bearish convictions. When they foresee a protracted market decline, they may initiate bearish positions by buying put options or employing more advanced strategies like bear spreads or ratio spreads. These positions profit if the index falls, aligning with their contrarian outlook.

3. Contrarian Analysis of Option Data: Contrarian investors dive deep into option data, analyzing factors such as open interest, volume, and the distribution of option strikes. Unusual option activity or a concentration of puts can provide valuable insights into market sentiment. Contrarians interpret this data in the context of their contrarian thesis, enhancing their decision-making process.

Mastering the art of timing with index options is an essential skill in the contrarian investor's toolkit. Recognizing contrarian signals within index movements, deciphering overbought and oversold conditions using index options, and strategically utilizing index put options for both hedging and contrarian bearish plays are all vital components of this art. Contrarian investing is not about mere contrariness; it's about precision, analysis, and the strategic use of instruments like index options to navigate the complex landscape of the financial markets.

## 10.3 Advanced Techniques with Index Options

In the realm of contrarian investing, mastering advanced techniques with index options can provide a formidable edge. Index options, which derive their value from broad market indices like the S&P 500 or the Dow Jones Industrial Average, offer unique opportunities and strategies for contrarian investors seeking to navigate the markets with precision. In this subchapter, we'll explore the intricacies of advanced techniques with index options, including risk-reduction strategies, income generation, and managing the ever-present beast of volatility.

### Spreads and Strategies for Reducing Risk

One of the key advantages of index options is their flexibility in constructing spread strategies that help contrarian investors mitigate risk while still participating in the market's movements. Here are some advanced techniques used by contrarian investors:

1. Vertical Spreads: Contrarian investors often employ vertical spreads, such as the bull put spread and bear call spread, to control risk. These strategies involve simultaneously buying and selling options of the same type (puts or calls) but with different strike prices. By doing so, contrarians can define their maximum loss while benefiting from limited profit potential.

2. Iron Condors: The iron condor strategy is a favorite among contrarians. It combines a bear call spread and a bull put spread on the same underlying index. This creates a range in which the index can trade without resulting in significant losses. Iron condors are ideal for sideways markets or when contrarians believe the market will remain within a certain range.

3. Ratio Spreads: For the more aggressive contrarian investor, ratio spreads can be employed. These involve an uneven number of options contracts on each side of the trade. For instance, a contrarian might sell two call options and buy one call option to reduce risk while still benefiting from price movement.

4. Collars: Contrarians concerned about downside risk may use collars. This strategy involves simultaneously buying a protective put option and selling a covered call option on an index position. It limits both potential gains and losses but provides peace of mind during market turbulence.

## Generating Income with Index Options

Contrarian investors recognize the importance of generating income, even in a contrarian investment strategy. Advanced techniques with index options offer ways to supplement income while remaining true to contrarian principles:

1. Covered Call Writing: Contrarian investors holding long positions in index ETFs can enhance their returns by writing covered calls. This strategy involves selling call options on the index ETFs they already own. If the market remains steady or declines slightly, the premiums earned from selling the calls provide an additional income stream.

2. Cash-Secured Puts: Contrarians who are willing to buy an index ETF at a lower price can use cash-secured puts to generate income. They sell put options and, if the index ETF's price drops below the strike price, they are obligated to purchase it. If not, they keep the premium received for selling the puts.

3. Credit Spreads: Credit spreads, such as the bear put spread or bull call spread, allow contrarians to receive premiums upfront while limiting their potential losses. These strategies can be used to generate income in markets with low volatility.

## Managing Volatility in Contrarian Index Options Trading

Volatility is a constant companion in the world of contrarian investing. Advanced contrarian investors understand that managing volatility is key to their success when trading index options. Here are strategies for tackling this challenge:

1. Volatility Skew Analysis: Contrarians often analyze the implied volatility skew, which is the difference in implied volatility between out-of-the-money and in-the-money options. By understanding this skew, they can identify potential mispricings and adjust their option strategies accordingly.

2. VIX-Based Strategies: The CBOE Volatility Index (VIX) measures market volatility and is sometimes referred to as the "fear gauge." Contrarians use VIX-based strategies, such as VIX call or put options, to hedge their portfolios during periods of expected volatility.

3. Dynamic Hedging: Advanced contrarian investors dynamically hedge their options positions as market conditions change. They adjust their positions in response to shifts in implied volatility or significant price movements, ensuring that their risk remains under control.

4. Long Vega Strategies: Contrarians who anticipate a significant change in market volatility may employ long Vega strategies. These strategies involve buying options that benefit from an increase in implied volatility, potentially profiting from market turbulence.

5. Rolling Options: When contrarian investors hold options positions that are nearing expiration, they may choose to roll their positions by closing the current options and opening new ones with later expiration dates. This allows

them to adapt to changing market conditions and extend their contrarian strategies.

Mastering advanced techniques with index options is a journey that requires dedication, ongoing learning, and a commitment to disciplined risk management. Contrarian investors who harness these strategies can not only navigate volatile markets but also extract substantial profits while staying true to their contrarian principles. Remember, in the world of contrarian investing, it's not just about swimming against the tide; it's about doing so with precision and finesse.

# Chapter 11: Exploring New Horizons in Contrarian Investing

## 11.1 Geographic Contrarian Opportunities

In the ever-connected global marketplace, the world of contrarian investing extends far beyond one's local stock exchange. As a contrarian investor, you have the opportunity to diversify your portfolio and tap into unique opportunities by exploring international markets. In this subchapter, we will embark on a journey to discover the world of geographic contrarian opportunities, unraveling the strategies, trends, and currency considerations that define this intriguing facet of contrarian investing.

### International Contrarian Investing Strategies

Contrarian investing knows no borders, and neither should your investment strategy. International markets offer a vast canvas for contrarian investors to paint their unique approach. Here are some strategies contrarians employ when venturing beyond their home turf:

1. Value Hunting Abroad: Contrarian investors seek undervalued assets in international markets. They look for countries or regions facing economic or political challenges that have caused their markets to slump. While others shy away from such uncertainty, contrarians see potential in these undervalued assets.

2. Global Sector Rotation: Contrarian investors often rotate their investments among different sectors in global markets. When a particular sector or industry is out of favor in one

country, contrarians may find opportunities in the same sector in another region.

3. Emerging Market Contrarianism: Emerging markets are ripe with contrarian opportunities. Contrarians may invest in countries experiencing temporary setbacks, such as economic crises or political turmoil, with an eye on long-term growth potential.

4. Contrarian ETFs: Exchange-traded funds (ETFs) offer an easy way to gain exposure to international markets. Contrarians may use ETFs that track specific regions or industries, allowing for diversified contrarian plays.

**Recognizing Contrarian Trends in Global Markets**
Contrarian investing on a global scale requires a keen eye for spotting trends that others overlook. Here are some key principles to help you identify contrarian opportunities in international markets:

1. Macroeconomic Factors: Contrarians pay attention to economic indicators such as GDP growth, inflation rates, and unemployment. When an economy is down and out, contrarians often see the potential for a turnaround.

2. Political Developments: Political instability can create market uncertainty, but contrarians are not deterred. They analyze political situations to assess whether market reactions are overblown or justified.

3. Market Sentiment: Contrarians monitor market sentiment in international regions. If pessimism prevails and markets

are oversold, contrarians may see an opportunity to buy low.

4. Currency Movements: Currency fluctuations can impact international investments. Contrarians may study currency trends to determine if they align with their contrarian thesis.

## Currency Considerations in International Contrarian Investing

When venturing into international contrarian investing, currencies become a critical consideration. Currency movements can significantly impact the return on your investments. Here's how contrarian investors navigate the complex world of currencies:

1. Hedging Strategies: Some contrarian investors use currency hedging strategies to mitigate the risk of adverse currency movements. Hedging involves entering contracts to offset potential currency losses.

2. Currency Diversification: Contrarians may diversify their currency exposure by holding investments in different currencies. This diversification helps spread currency risk.

3. Monitoring Exchange Rates: Constant monitoring of exchange rates is essential. Contrarians keep a close eye on currency trends and news that may affect exchange rates.

4. Impact on Investment Decisions: Contrarians factor currency considerations into their investment decisions. If they anticipate a currency strengthening, they may consider investments in that region more attractive.

5. Long-Term Currency Trends: Contrarian investors assess long-term currency trends. They seek to align their international investments with currencies they believe will appreciate over time.

## The Contrarian's Global Playground

In the ever-evolving landscape of contrarian investing, geographic diversification is a tool that can enhance your ability to find value and seize opportunities. By venturing into international markets, you broaden your perspective and gain exposure to a diverse array of industries, economies, and political climates.

But remember, international contrarian investing comes with its own set of challenges. Diverse regulations, time zones, and cultural differences require thorough research and due diligence. Each country has its unique risk factors, and the political and economic climate can change rapidly.

Successful international contrarian investing requires a blend of astute analysis, risk management, and adaptability. It's not about blindly investing in foreign markets but about using contrarian principles to uncover hidden gems and recognize value where others may not.

As you explore geographic contrarian opportunities, approach each investment with the same rigor and discipline that define contrarian investing. Analyze the fundamentals, assess the contrarian potential, and keep a watchful eye on currency dynamics. In doing so, you'll expand your contrarian toolkit and open doors to a world of investment possibilities, all guided by the contrarian's unwavering principle: the courage to be different when it matters most.

## 11.2 Emerging Sectors and Contrarian Potential

In the ever-evolving world of contrarian investing, one of the most exciting frontiers lies in exploring emerging sectors. While contrarian strategies have traditionally been associated with undervalued stocks and assets, the modern contrarian investor recognizes that opportunities extend far beyond the established norms. In this subchapter, we delve into the uncharted territories of contrarian investing, focusing on the identification of niche sectors with contrarian appeal, strategies for navigating the complex landscape of emerging technologies, and the promising prospects of green and renewable energy.

### Identifying Niche Sectors with Contrarian Appeal

Contrarian investing is about being different, but it's also about recognizing where the crowd might be overlooking opportunities. Emerging sectors often serve as fertile ground for contrarians. Here's how contrarian investors identify niche sectors with contrarian appeal:

1. Investigate Market Neglect: Contrarians seek sectors that have been overshadowed by more popular investments.

This neglect can lead to undervaluation, providing contrarians with entry points that others have missed.

2. Scrutinize Long-Term Fundamentals: While emerging sectors may exhibit volatility, contrarians look beyond short-term fluctuations. They assess the long-term fundamentals of a sector, including its growth potential, competitive advantages, and market dynamics.

3. Consider Contrarian Catalysts: Contrarian investors watch for catalysts that could shift sentiment and drive interest in a neglected sector. These catalysts might include regulatory changes, technological breakthroughs, or shifts in consumer preferences.

## Contrarian Strategies in Emerging Technologies
The world of technology is a breeding ground for contrarian opportunities. As innovation accelerates, emerging technologies often face skepticism and uncertainty, creating fertile ground for contrarian investors. Here are some contrarian strategies tailored to navigating the complex world of emerging tech:

1. Deep Dive Due Diligence: Contrarians dig deep into the technologies they consider. This involves not only understanding the technology itself but also the competitive landscape, potential disruptors, and the challenges it seeks to address.

2. Growth vs. Value Assessment: Emerging tech companies often prioritize growth over profitability in their early stages. Contrarians carefully assess whether the growth

potential justifies the current valuation or if the market has become overly optimistic.

3. Diversification within Tech: Rather than putting all their eggs in one tech basket, contrarian investors diversify their tech investments. They recognize that not all tech startups will succeed, and diversification spreads risk.

4. Timing the Hype Cycle: Emerging tech sectors often experience hype cycles, marked by periods of irrational exuberance followed by disillusionment. Contrarians aim to enter when the hype subsides but before the genuine potential is fully realized.

**Capitalizing on Trends in Green and Renewable Energy**

The global shift towards sustainability and green energy presents a promising frontier for contrarian investors. As the world seeks eco-friendly alternatives to traditional energy sources, contrarians are finding opportunities in renewable energy. Here's how contrarians capitalize on green energy trends:

1. Long-Term Energy Transition: Contrarian investors recognize that the transition to green energy is not a short-term trend but a long-term global shift. They invest with a multi-year horizon, understanding that the full potential of renewable energy may take time to materialize.

2. Analyzing Sub-Sectors: Within the green energy sector, contrarians analyze sub-sectors, such as solar, wind, hydro,

and electric vehicles. Each sub-sector has its unique dynamics and potential contrarian opportunities.

3. Government Policy Impact: Contrarian investors closely monitor government policies and incentives related to green energy. Subsidies, tax credits, and regulations can significantly impact the profitability of green energy companies.

4. Evaluating ESG Considerations: Contrarians incorporate environmental, social, and governance (ESG) factors into their analysis. Companies with strong ESG practices are often better positioned for long-term success in the green energy sector.

Consider a contrarian investor who identifies an undervalued renewable energy company in the midst of a market downturn. While others are fleeing, this contrarian sees potential. They conduct thorough research on the company's technology, financials, and competitive advantages.

Recognizing the long-term trend toward renewable energy and the company's commitment to sustainability, the contrarian invests with a horizon of several years. They understand that market sentiment may not immediately align with the company's true value.

Over time, as the world continues to embrace renewable energy solutions, the market catches up to the contrarian's thesis. The previously undervalued stock begins to appreciate, and the contrarian investor reaps the rewards of their foresight and patience.

Contrarian investing is not confined to the familiar realms of undervalued stocks and traditional assets. It extends into uncharted territories, where emerging sectors and technologies present unique contrarian opportunities. By identifying niche sectors with contrarian appeal, navigating emerging tech landscapes with due diligence, and capitalizing on the green energy revolution, contrarian investors can expand their horizons and discover new avenues for potential profit.

As you venture into these unexplored frontiers of contrarian investing, remember that the same principles of patience, discipline, and rigorous analysis still apply. While the terrain may be different, the contrarian spirit remains constant, driving you to seek opportunities where others fear to tread. In the ever-changing world of finance, the contrarian investor stands as a beacon of independence and innovation, ready to seize opportunities wherever they may arise.

# Conclusion

As we draw the curtains on our exploration of contrarian investing, it's essential to reflect on the insights, strategies, and principles we've uncovered throughout this journey. Contrarian investing is not merely a financial strategy; it's a philosophy—a way of thinking and approaching the complex world of finance and investment with a unique perspective. In this conclusion, we'll revisit the key takeaways and provide you with a roadmap for applying contrarian investing principles in your financial endeavors.

## The Contrarian's Mindset

Contrarian investing begins with cultivating the contrarian's mindset. It's about challenging the prevailing wisdom and being willing to stand alone when the crowd is headed in the opposite direction. At its core, this mindset revolves around a few critical principles:

1. Rational Skepticism: Contrarians approach the markets with a healthy dose of skepticism. They understand that market sentiment can be irrational and that trends often overshoot fundamentals. By questioning the consensus, contrarians identify opportunities where others see only risks.

2. Independent Thinking: Contrarian investors prize independent thinking. They don't follow the herd; they chart their course based on their analysis and convictions.

This independent thinking allows them to uncover hidden gems that others overlook.

3. Long-Term Perspective: Contrarians have a long-term perspective. They aren't swayed by short-term fluctuations or market noise. Instead, they focus on the fundamental value of assets and their potential for long-term growth.

4. Emotional Discipline: Emotional discipline is the cornerstone of contrarian success. Fear and greed drive market sentiment, but contrarians remain steadfast in the face of these emotions. They buy when others are fearful and sell when others are greedy.

The toolbox of contrarian investing comprises a blend of technical and fundamental analysis, sentiment analysis, and unique contrarian indicators. Together, these tools empower contrarians to make informed decisions, identify market extremes, and seize opportunities when the crowd is either overly optimistic or excessively pessimistic.

Timing plays a pivotal role in contrarian investing. By understanding market cycles and their interplay with contrarian strategies, investors can discern when to exercise caution, when to acquire undervalued assets, and when to exercise patience. The use of technical and fundamental analysis, coupled with contrarian indicators, enables precise timing of entry and exit points, maximizing the potential for profit.

Managing risk is another cornerstone of contrarian investing. Diversification, stop-loss orders, careful position sizing, continuous monitoring, and unwavering discipline collectively form a robust risk management framework. By adhering to these principles, contrarians protect their capital and maintain the resilience required to weather market fluctuations.

As you embark on your own contrarian investing journey, consider the roadmap we've laid out. Begin by defining your financial goals and risk tolerance, aligning your strategy accordingly. Continue to educate yourself, for the world of finance is ever-evolving. Cultivate patience and discipline, and be prepared for a journey that may not yield immediate results. Adapt and learn from your experiences, and remain committed to the principles of contrarian investing.

In closing, contrarian investing is a profound journey that calls for intellectual rigor, emotional resilience, and unwavering dedication to your convictions. By navigating financial markets through the lens of contrarianism, you join the ranks of some of history's most successful investors. While the path may at times be solitary, the wisdom and principles you've gleaned from this book will be your steadfast companions.

Armed with knowledge, a contrarian mindset, and a diverse set of tools, you stand poised to embark on your own contrarian investing adventure. The world of finance beckons, eager to receive your unique perspective, your independent thought, and your courage to diverge from the norm. May your contrarian journey be both prosperous and fulfilling, and may your profits stand as a testament to the extraordinary potential that lies beyond conventional thinking in the world of finance.